100s
of Fun Things to
Make and Do

100s
of Fun Things to Make and Do

Susie Johns

p

This is a Parragon Publishing Book

This edition published in 2003

Parragon Publishing
Queen Street House
4 Queen Street
Bath BA1 1HE, UK

Copyright © Parragon 2002

Designed, produced and packaged by
Stonecastle Graphics Limited

Text by Susie Johns
Craft items and cookery by Susie Johns
Edited by Gillian Haslam
Designed by Sue Pressley and Paul Turner
Photography by Roddy Paine

ISBN 1-40540-452-3

Printed in China

Disclaimer

This book is fun and will provide many hours
of inspiration for children of all ages. Safety
is very important. Young children should
always be supervized by a responsible adult
when making the craft items, or food and
drinks described in this book. Care should
be taken with scissors, knives, and other
sharp objects, and before commencing with
any project you are advised to ensure the
worksurface is protected. Always read the
instructions supplied with paints and dyes
etc., as they may differ from those given in
this book. The publisher and their agents
cannot accept liability for any loss, damage
or injury however caused.

Contents

Toys and Games

Contents

Introduction

Home-made toys and games are double the fun – fun to make as well as being fun to play with. Here are some new ideas and some variations on traditional favorites, all easy to make.

A load of old junk!

It is surprising what you can create with things that may just be lying around the house. Make a point of collecting together cardboard boxes, including shoe boxes with separate lids, scraps of paper and cardboard, pieces of fabric and felt, dried beans or rice, plastic bags, plastic bottles, string and knitting yarn, paper clips and rubber bands, canisters from cocoa or curry powder, old newspapers – and even odd socks and gloves!

You may need to buy a few things such as soft toy batting and bells – but the chances are you will be able to get hold of all the other stuff for free. Just ask around! Build up a box full of basic materials that can be used in all your creative projects. These will include paints and brushes, glue, sticky tape, scissors, needle and thread, ruler, pens, and pencils.

A helping hand

If you follow the instructions carefully, and refer to the pictures of the finished projects, you should have no trouble at all in making any or all of the items featured in *Toys and Games*.

Occasionally, if you get stuck, you may have to ask someone for help. You are certainly advized to seek adult assistance when it comes to tricky techniques such as cutting a hole in thick cardboard, where a craft knife may be more useful than a pair of scissors. Or when it comes to sewing, an adult may have more experience and will be able to give you some tips.

Here are some basic tips and techniques to refer to if you get stuck...

Papier mâché

By mixing glue and paper you can produce a hard–wearing shell that will stand up to hours and hours of play. Papier mâché is usually built up on some kind of framework, such as a cardboard model. Construct the framework from pieces cut from a strong cardboard box, holding it all together with plenty of sticky tape.

Dilute some white craft glue with an equal amount of water in a plastic cup or a jelly jar. Stir it well and you should have a mixture resembling heavy cream or milk shake. If it is too thick, you can always stir in a little more water.

Brush this mixture all over your model, then apply pieces of newspaper, torn into strips. If the cardboard you have used for the basic construction is thick and sturdy, you should only need to cover it with about three layers of paper and glue to make the finished model nice and strong.

Sometimes papier mâché is built up on a flimsier base. For instance, if you use a balloon as your basic shape, you will need to build up at least seven or eight layers of glue and paper because, once the balloon is burst, the papier mâché shell needs to be really strong and thick, or it will become dented or may even crumple and collapse.

Sewing

All the stitching in these projects is simple. Even if you have not done much – or any – sewing before, it should not be too difficult.

If, however, you don't like sewing, some items, such as the finger puppets, can simply be glued together. Use a special fabric glue or white craft glue, spread very thinly so it does not soak into the fabric or felt.

Paints

The models pictured in *Toys and Games* have been painted with acrylics. You can use poster paints, if you already have these. However, you may have to varnish your painted model to protect it. Use a water-based varnish or simply brush with the same white craft glue and water mixture you used for the papier mâché. This will dry to a transparent, slightly shiny, protective finish which will make the item more hard-wearing.

Acrylic paints are recommended, however, as they are easy to use, colorful, and will give a good finish to your models, without the need for varnishing. Try them if you haven't done so already!

9

Fabric Juggling Balls

These are easier to catch than a ball as they don't roll away. If you are learning to juggle, make a set of three.

You will need:
fabric scraps
needle and thread
dried beans, rice, or lentils

1 Cut the fabric scraps into 4 inch squares.

2 Place two squares of fabric, in contrasting colors, together, and sew along three sides, approximately 1/4 inch from the edges.

3 Turn right sides out and pour in dried beans, lentils, or rice until bags are three-quarters full.

4 Fold in raw edges on the open side. Place folded edges together and stitch the opening closed.

Bean bag people

As with the fabric juggling balls, you will need fabric scraps. Cut two identical shapes for the head and body. It helps to draw the shape of your bean bag person on paper first. When you are satisfied with the shape, cut it out and use it as a template for cutting fabric. Stitch the fabric for the head to the body fabric, then with wrong sides facing outward, stitch the front and back together. Leave a small gap so you can turn it right sides out. Fill three-quarters full with beans or lentils and stitch the opening closed. Draw features on the face with a permanent marker pen.

Rubber juggling balls

These colorful juggling balls are quick and easy to make from balloons and rice. As well as being great for juggling, why not use them for any ball game or for throwing at targets such as skittles.

You will need:
small plastic bags
rice
balloons
scissors

1 Place about two tablespoons of rice in a plastic bag and knot it tightly, to seal.

2 Cut the neck off a balloon and push the rice-filled bag inside. Cut the neck off a second balloon and stretch it over the first in the same way.

Toy Theater

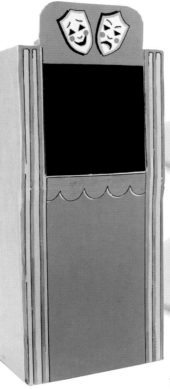

A basic puppet theater, constructed from cardboard boxes, can be adapted for different kinds of puppets – construct the basic shape then customize it any way you like!

You will need:
2 cardboard boxes, approximately the same size
sticky tape
white craft glue
newspapers
paints

The theater pictured has been constructed from wine boxes. The cardboard divisions for the wine bottles have been left in place in the base box, to help strengthen the construction. These also act as handy storage for puppets and props, so the theater can easily be tidied away.

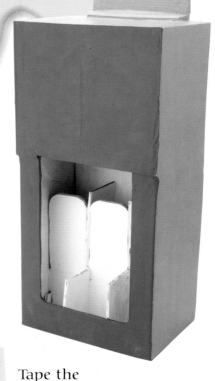

1 Stand one box on top of the other. Decide where you want your puppets to appear and cut away the appropriate areas. For instance, if you are using finger or hand puppets, cut a large, square hole in the back of the base box, and another in the top. For string puppets, you do not need to cut any holes in the base, but you will need to cut away the top of the upper box. In any case, cut a large hole in the front of the upper box, so your audience can see the show!

2 Tape the boxes together firmly. Tape down any flaps and cover up any holes. Cut a shape from spare cardboard and tape it to the top, as a decorative touch.

3 Mix white craft glue with water to the consistency of heavy cream and tear newspaper into strips. Use the glue and paper to cover the whole construction in a couple of layers of papier mâché to make it strong and durable. Pay particular attention to the corners and edges. Leave to dry.

4 Have fun painting the theater. You can just paint it black, or you could paint columns up each side and theatrical masks above the stage. It is up to you.

Customize your own theater

If you want to be really elaborate, you could make drapes for your theater and use battery-operated torches to light the stage. To make drapes, cut rectangles of fabric to fit the opening at the front. Hem these and fold over some fabric at the top, stitching to form a tunnel that can be threaded with string or wire. The wire should be stretched across the top of the stage, inside or outside the box, whichever is easier. Use paper clips or lengths of ribbon to hold back the drapes during performances.

13

Make a sock puppet

Cut across the toe of a sock, then cut slits about 4cm long on either side.

Cut an oval of pink felt to fit the hole you have made and stitch this in place to form the mouth. Stitch on circles of white and black felt for eyes and a strip of red felt for a tongue.

Puppet Parade

Paint a wooden spoon with a happy/sad face, customize an odd glove into a furry monster, or create a whole cast of finger puppet characters to act out your favorite stories.

Finger puppets

You can make all kinds of finger puppet characters: kings and queens, angels, sailors, or even Father Christmas. All you need are scraps of colored felt, a needle and thread, and lots of imagination.

You will need:
colored felt
scissors
needle and thread

1 Using the puppets pictured here as a guide, cut out shapes for bodies, hands, feet, and other features. The body can be a simple rectangle – place your finger on a piece of felt and draw around it, then add a bit extra all round so it will fit once it has been stitched. Or you can add arms to the basic shape.

2 Choose which piece will be the front part of the body then stitch on head, hands, and other details.

3 Stitch the front part of the body to the back, leaving the bottom edge open so you can fit your finger inside.

Wooden spoon puppet

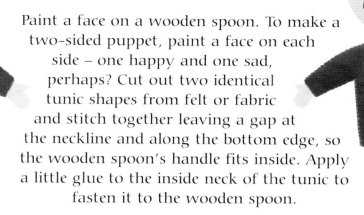

Paint a face on a wooden spoon. To make a two-sided puppet, paint a face on each side – one happy and one sad, perhaps? Cut out two identical tunic shapes from felt or fabric and stitch together leaving a gap at the neckline and along the bottom edge, so the wooden spoon's handle fits inside. Apply a little glue to the inside neck of the tunic to fasten it to the wooden spoon.

Glove puppet

Stitch the three middle fingers of a glove together. Do this by stitching up the sides of the fingers – you will still need to get your hand inside.

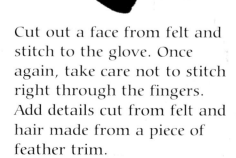

Cut out a face from felt and stitch to the glove. Once again, take care not to stitch right through the fingers. Add details cut from felt and hair made from a piece of feather trim.

15

Traditional Games

Test your powers of concentration and your strategic skills with a game of checkers, chess, or tic tac toe. But before you do – why not make your own game board and counters, so you can also show off your creative ability!

Checkers/chessboard

This board is simply made from the lid of a large cardboard box. If you cannot find a suitable lid, you could cut the base from a cardboard box, leaving a small rim all round, or simply paint a large sheet of cardboard. The counters pictured are made from wooden discs. You could just as easily use painted bottle tops or circles cut from cardboard.

You will need:
large cardboard box lid or sheet of cardboard
white emulsion paint (optional)
acrylic paints
paintbrushes
ruler and pencil
32 wooden or cardboard discs
colored paper
white craft glue

1 Paint the inside of the box lid with white acrylic or emulsion paint. When dry, measure and mark out the squares for the board and paint them in your choice of colors. The board needs to be eight squares by eight squares.

2 Paint half the discs one color and half a contrasting color. When the paint is dry, cut out shapes from paper and glue them on to one side of the counters, to make chess pieces. Leave the other side of each counter blank, for playing checkers.

16

3D noughts and crosses

Otherwise known as tic tac toe, this game is usually played with pencils and paper. This papier mâché version is not only fun to play with, but also fun to make from scraps of cardboard and newspaper.

You will need:
cardboard
ruler
scissors
sticky tape
white craft glue
newspapers
10 wooden or cardboard discs
acrylic paints
paintbrushes

1 Cut eight strips of cardboard measuring 7 x $\frac{5}{8}$ inch. Form four strips into a grid, fixing them together with sticky tape where they overlap. Add a second layer of strips on top, binding them tightly to the first layer with sticky tape, to form a rigid base.

2 Dilute white craft glue with a little water and brush all over the cardboard base, then apply torn strips of newspaper, winding them round to cover the edges of the cardboard and brushing with more diluted white craft glue. Build up about three or four layers of newspaper in this way, then leave to dry.

3 Meanwhile, paint five discs one color and the other five a contrasting color and leave to dry. Paint a cross on top of five of the disks and a nought on the other five.

4 Paint the papier mâché grid, using any color you like. You may wish to outline the edges in black or a contrasting color. Leave to dry.

17

Target Games

Fun to play on a rainy day or great for a party. Enjoy constructing and painting these simple games – and then enjoy playing them!

Aunt Sally

Here is a table-top version of an old fairground game that is easy to make from a single piece of cardboard and can be stored flat, so will take up very little space. Copy the face or make up your own – a clown, perhaps, or an animal such as a lion?

You will need:
cardboard box
ruler
scissors
acrylic paints
paintbrushes

1 Cut a rectangle measuring 20 x 8 inches from a cardboard box, making sure that a fold runs across it, about 8 inches from one of the shorter ends, to form a hinge. This 8 inch square forms the base.

2 Draw a face with a big mouth on the larger portion of the cardboard. Cut out the mouth and paint the face using acrylic paints. Paint the reverse of the card, too.

3 To play the game, place a bowl or cup on the shorter end of the card and prop the larger portion against it. Throw crumpled balls of paper at the target, aiming for the mouth, and decide how many points to award for every ball that lands in the cup.

Tiddlywinks

This is quick to make, fun to play, and
pocket-sized so you can carry it with you.

1 Cut a 4 inch square of thick
cardboard. Draw a star
shape with a circle in the
center. Paint the design or
use paper cutouts stuck
on to the card.

2 Place a small cup
or bottle top in
the center then,
using a large tiddlywink
to press and flick the
smaller counters, aim
for the cup.

3 Decide on a
scoring system
– 5 points for
landing on the star and 10 points
for getting the tiddlywink into the
cup, perhaps?

Target box

1 Draw a series of circles,
like a target, on the lid
of a box.

2 Cut out the center
circle and paint the
other rings in different
colors, using acrylic paints.

3 Paint on
numbers,
or cut
these out from
paper and stick
in place.

1
3
5
10

4 Lie the box flat and throw
crumpled balls of paper or
aluminum foil, aiming for
the hole in the center but scoring
points for any balls that land on
the numbered rings.

Ball Games

Fun to play alone or you can challenge your friends. Here are two games to test your aim, plus some ideas for making balls.

Bottle ball catcher

1 Cut a plastic bottle in half and discard the base. Bind the cut edge of the top with sticky tape.

2 Tie a 28 inch length of string to the bottle neck, just below the cap, and attach the other end of the string to a paper clip stuck into a papier mâché ball.

Papier mâché ball

1 Start with a polystyrene ball, or simply crumple a sheet of newspaper into a tight ball and bind it with sticky tape.

2 Then cover the ball with papier mâché, by brushing with diluted white craft glue and building up four layers of torn newspaper strips.

3 Leave it to dry and then paint a colorful design using acrylic paints.

Rubber band ball

Great for throwing at targets and easy to make. Use rubber bands wrapped one on top of another to form a bouncy ball.

Hoop-la

Glue a cardboard tube to a square of thick cardboard. If you wish, you can cover the whole thing with several layers of papier mâché, then paint and decorate with shiny sticky tape. Throw curtain rings or plastic bangles and try to get them over the tube.

Games to Play

Use your home-made balls to play some of the games you will find on other pages.

A papier mâché ball is perfect for indoor fun as it is light – just right for throwing at a target such as the Aunt Sally or the Target Box. Or line up a set of Can Skittles and try to throw the ball so it lands inside, scoring the number written on the can!

The rubber band ball is slightly heavier and quite bouncy. Bounce it at the Target Box or roll it to try to knock down your home-made skittles.

Gone Fishing

Make a shoal of paper fish, then try to catch them with a home-made fishing rod. You can put a magnet on the end of your fishing line or a hook – it's up to you.

You will need:
metallic silver cardboard
poster paints
paintbrush
scissors
paperclips
wooden stick
string or cord
magnet or paperclip

22

Crafty tip
To play the game, place the fish in a box lid or plastic bowl – or why not cut a pond shape from corrugated cardboard?

1 Paint the cardboard with a layer of thick poster paint in one or two colors. Before the paint is dry, use the other end of the paintbrush to scratch fish shapes. Leave to dry.

2 Cut out the fish shapes and attach a paperclip to each one.

3 Tie a length of string to one end of the stick. Tie a magnet or a paperclip bent into a hook at the other end of the string.

Flying fish

This Japanese-style kite is simply made from tissue paper and string. Perfect for a breezy day, it is

probably too delicate to fly in very strong winds.

You will need:
tissue paper
colored inks
plate
very wide brush or sponge
fine paintbrush
glue stick
paper scraps
hole punch
string

23

1 Place sheets of tissue paper on a layer of newspaper. Pour a little ink on to a plate, dip in the brush or sponge, and brush stripes of color across the tissue paper. Leave to dry.

2 Use paint and a fine brush to paint a fish shape on one sheet of tissue paper, and details such as fins and scales. Leave to dry then place this upside down under a second sheet of tissue and draw another fish, this time in reverse, for the other side of the kite.

3 With the glue stick, draw a thin line of glue all around the edge of one of the fish, on the reverse side. Do not apply glue to openings at mouth and tail. Place this sheet on the second sheet, matching up the fish outlines, press down and, when the glue is dry, cut out.

4 Cut four small squares of paper and glue them back to back on each side of the fish kite's mouth. Punch a hole in each one and thread with a short length of string, tying one end to each hole. Tie the end of a longer length of string to the center of the first piece.

Character Skittles

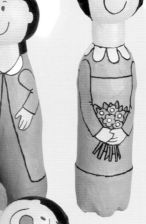

Save empty plastic bottles from soft drinks to make a set of skittles. Here are four funny characters but you could make as many as you like. For indoor play, use a soft ball to try to knock them over.

You will need:
plastic bottles
sticky tape
polystyrene balls
(optional)
newspaper
white craft glue
acrylic paints
paintbrushes

24

1 Before you start, you may wish to pour a small amount of water into each of the bottles, so they do not tip over too easily. Screw on the lids really tightly and bind with sticky tape.

2 Glue a polystyrene ball to the top of each bottle. If you do not have any, just crumple a sheet of newspaper into a tight ball and use this for the head.

3 Dilute some white craft glue with water to the consistency of heavy cream and brush all over the bottle and the ball. Cover with torn newspaper strips – at least four layers but preferably five or six, to make the skittles really tough.

4 When the papier mâché is dry, paint the skittles, using your imagination to create funny faces and costumes.

Can skittles

Save canisters from coffee, drinking chocolate, and savory snacks. Paint them with brightly colored acrylic paints, adding painted numbers for scoring. Stack up the cans and try to knock them down by throwing a ball at them. Score the appropriate number of points for every can you knock over.

25

Carry Boxes

Transform a cardboard bottle carrier into a strong, portable storage box for your fashion dolls or action heroes and all their accessories and equipment.

You will need:
cardboard wine carrier
scrap cardboard
sticky tape
white craft glue
torn newspaper strips
acrylic paints
paintbrush
marker pen
glitter (optional)

1 Trim off any flaps or bits from the box that you do not want. If the box has open ends, cut cardboard shapes to fit and tape in place.

2 Dilute white craft glue with water to the consistency of heavy cream and brush all over the outside of the box. Then cover it with about three or four layers of torn newspaper strips. Pay particular attention to edges and joins, to make the finished box really strong. Leave the box to dry.

3 Paint the box, inside and out, with your chosen base color, then, when this is dry, paint it all over with your chosen color scheme.

For fashion dolls, a bright base color such as pink is perfect! Add designs on top, in other colors and, when dry, outline these with a permanent marker pen. For added sparkle, apply lines of white craft glue and sprinkle with glitter.

For action dolls, try a camouflage effect. Choose one color for the base, such as a light olive green, then add broad areas of other shades of green and brown.

27

For a collection of cuddly animals, choose bright primary colors. Paint the bottom part of the box yellow, the top red to look like a roof, and the inside bright blue. You could even add painted labels with each pet's name written in permanent marker pen!

Music Makers

You don't need to be a maestro – with a collection of bits and pieces found around the house, you can make marvelous music!

Box guitar

For an instant guitar, stretch rubber bands over a box. You could use a cardboard shoe box or chocolate box, or a small wooden box. To adjust the sound of each string, try inserting some matches. To play the guitar, pluck the strings with your fingertips.

Glass bottle xylophone

Part fill clean glass bottles with water. Add a few drops of food coloring, if you like. If you arrange eight bottles in a row and adjust the water levels carefully, you can produce a musical scale and play tunes.

Drum sticks

Push one end of a wooden stick into a large wooden bead. Make a pair of sticks and decorate them with acrylic paints, then use them to tap out tunes on your bottle xylophone.

Maracas

If you like salsa music, here is the very thing for you – a pair of colorful maracas that you can shake to the rhythm.

Crafty Tips
You can fill these shakers with rice, dried beans, crumpled balls of aluminum foil, or paper clips. Try different things for a different sound.

You will need:
2 cardboard tubes
2 balloons
white craft glue
newspapers
string
rice, beans or lentils (see Crafty tips)
acrylic paints
paintbrushes

1 Cover the cardboard tubes with three layers of papier mâché. To do this, brush the tubes with white craft glue diluted to the consistency of heavy cream and add torn strips of newspaper. Leave aside to dry.

2 Meanwhile, pour some rice into each balloon, then inflate and knot the end. Cover each balloon with at least six or seven layers of papier mâché. Attach a length of string to each one and hang up to dry.

3 When the papier mâché is dry, burst the balloons and remove them from the papier mâché shells. Push one end of each tube into a balloon and add two more layers of papier mâché to cover the join. Leave to dry.

29

4 Paint the maracas in colorful designs.

Jingle Jangle

Here are some musical makes that are sure to get you moving, with bells on your ankles, a jingle stick to shake, and a tambourine to beat out the rhythm of the dance!

Jingle stick

Decorate a cardboard tube with paints, colored sticky tape or sticky labels. Make holes in one end and use lengths of thin wire or strong thread to attach clusters of bells. Shake the stick in time to the music!

Jingle jangle

Cut strips of felt long enough to go around your wrists or ankles, with about 1 inch overlap. Stitch on bells and stitch a snap fastener to the ends. Wear these round your wrists and ankles when you dance!

Tambourine

Save cheese boxes with lids to make a jingling tambourine. Paint it with bright colors and patterns. You can even add ribbon streamers for extra color and movement! To play the tambourine, tap it with your hand or a drumstick.

You will need:
round cheese box with lid
gummed brown paper
parcel tape
paints
paintbrushes
bells or bottle tops
string or ribbon

 Make holes in the rim of the box base and corresponding holes in the lid. Replace the lid so the holes line up, then tape the lid in place, using strips of brown parcel tape.

2 Paint the box all over with bright patterns.

3 Attach bells or bottle tops using lengths of string or ribbon.

Crafty tips
If you are using bottle tops you will need to make holes. Do this by placing the bottle top on a piece of wood and banging a nail through with a hammer. Ask an adult to help with this. Be careful of the sharp edges.

31

Soft Toys

Scraps of fabric, needle and thread, and some soft stuffing are all you need to make a collection of cuddly toys. Use fabrics that are nice to touch, such as natural cotton or soft velvet and practice your sewing skills.

You will need:
pieces of cotton fabric, at least
10 x 6 inches
needle and thread
polyester stuffing
rattle (optional – see Crafty tips)

Fabric ball

This squashy ball is soft enough for indoor play. Made from scraps of colorful cotton fabric, stitched together and stuffed with a soft filling, it's easier to make than you might think, and safe enough for a toddler, but do not give it to a baby.

1 Enlarge templates A and B to twice their size (or larger). This is easy to do on a photocopier. Use them to cut out shapes from fabric. You will need four of shape A and eight of shape B.

2 Stitch together one shape A and two shapes Bs, to make a segment. Repeat until you have four segments. With each one, leave a gap for stuffing, stuff firmly, and stitch the opening closed.

Crafty tips
To add an extra dimension to your ball, put a rattle inside when you are stuffing one of the segments. To make a rattle, place a few beads or dried beans, or a small bell, inside a plastic film canister.

Flat cat

Cut two identical cat shapes from velvet. On one, stitch on eyes, ears, and nose cut from colored felt. With black thread in your needle, stitch a mouth shape. Now, with the velvety sides of the fabric together, stitch all round, leaving a small gap so you can turn your cat inside out. Push stuffing through the gap, then sew the gap closed. To give the cat jointed arms and legs, stitch across through all thicknesses of fabric.

You will need:
pieces of velvet
needle and thread
polyester stuffing

3 Stitch two of the segments together, by joining the pointed ends. Do the same with the other pair but at the same time, join the ends to the top and bottom of the first pair. To hide these joins you can tie a length of ribbon around the ends. Do not give the ball to a baby.

33

Fabric ball templates

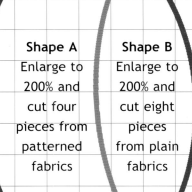

A

B

Shape A
Enlarge to 200% and cut four pieces from patterned fabrics

Shape B
Enlarge to 200% and cut eight pieces from plain fabrics

Odd Socks

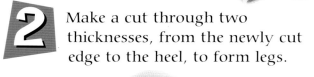

You will need:
1 sock
needle and thread
polyester toy batting
felt scraps
scrap of white terrycloth
safety pin
small piece of fabric
lace trimming
narrow ribbon

Every so often, a sock disappears into the depths of the washing machine and you are left with an odd one. Instead of throwing it away, transform it into a toy!

Sock baby

Even if you are inexperienced with a needle and thread, you can make this soft toy, for yourself or a smaller person.

34

1 Cut off the top of the sock, about 3 inches from the edge. Cut this piece in half, lengthwise, to make the arms.

2 Make a cut through two thicknesses, from the newly cut edge to the heel, to form legs.

3 Start stuffing the sock, pressing the batting into the toe. With needle and thread, stitch all round the sock, about 3¹/₂ inches from the toe end, and pull the thread up tightly, to form the head.

4 Tucking the cut edges inside, sew up the legs. Finish stuffing the body and legs, and stitch the ends of the legs closed.

5 Stitch the long edges of each arm piece together, stuff, then sew the open end of each one to the body.

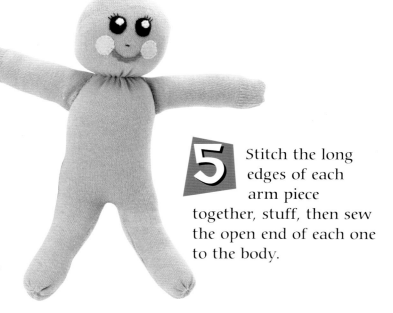

Sock hat for soft toy

Another odd sock makes a woolly hat for your favorite soft toy. Simply cut 4 inches from the ankle part of the sock. The ribbed edge can be folded up to form the brim of the hat. Stitch the cut edge, gathering it up to make the crown of the hat, then finish off with a woolly pom pom.

How to make a pom pom

Draw two 6cm circles on a piece of thin cardboard, and a $2^{1/2}$ inch circle in the center of each. Cut them out. Place these cardboard rings together and wind round and round with knitting yarn. When the rings are completely covered with a thick layer of yarn, cut the yarn between the outer edges of the rings, slip a length of yarn between the two rings, and tie tightly. Slip the rings off, then trim the woolly ball with scissors, to neaten it.

6 Cut out features from felt and stitch in place to make a face.

7 Cut out a square of white terrycloth, fold it into a triangle, and pin in place, to make a diaper.

8 Stitch the lace to one edge of a rectangle of fabric and wrap around the head, to make a bonnet. Trim to size, hem any raw edges, and tie in place with two lengths of narrow ribbon.

Noah's Ark

This boat, made from papier mâché, is strong enough to be played with again and again and, being hollow, is the ideal place to store and display a collection of model animals.

You will need:
cardboard box, such as shoe box
ruler and pencil
corrugated cardboard
scissors
sticky tape
cardboard box card
white craft glue
newspapers
acrylic paints
paintbrushes

1 Measure the height of the sides of your box and draw two long rectangles, the same width as this measurement, on corrugated cardboard. These will form the two sides of the ark. With your pencil, draw curved lines at either end, to form the bow and stern of the boat. Cut these shapes out and tape to the sides of the box. Tape together at each end.

2 Place the model upright on a sheet of cardboard cut from a strong cardboard box and draw around it. Cut out this shape, to form the base. Now cut two triangular shapes to cover the gaps at either end of the boat and two narrow strips to form the side decks.

3 Now measure the opening in the center of the boat and cut out shapes to form the four walls of a cabin that will fit on top of this opening. Tape in place.

4 Glue on rectangles of cardboard to form the door and windows and, lastly, cut two rectangles to form the sloping roof. Tape the roof pieces together but keep it separate from the rest of the boat.

5 Cover the model with at least four layers of papier mâché. Dilute white craft glue with water to the consistency of heavy cream. Brush it all over the cardboard model, inside and out, and cover with torn newspaper strips. Leave to dry.

6 Paint the whole model with white emulsion or acrylic and, when dry, paint the ark with bright colors.

Mr and Mrs Noah

Clothes pin doll people are perfect for
your home-made ark. Start
with old-fashioned wooden
pins, paint on faces, glue on
strands of knitting yarn for hair and
beards, and wrap with fabric scraps,
stitched or glued in place, for clothes.

Art Gallery

contents

Introduction

Everyone has the ability to draw. Being good at it just takes a bit of practice! And there are lots of ways to make pictures, besides painting and drawing – *Art Gallery* will show you how! Arm yourself with pencils, paper, paint, and glue and be prepared to make some marvellous pictures!

If you are stuck for picture-making inspiration, there are plenty of ideas to get you going on the following pages. But once you have mastered some of the techniques, remember that there is subject matter all around you. Create pictures of your family, your house, your pets, your possessions, or make patterns and shapes. Use pencil and paper, or paint, or have a go at printing. Or get really stuck in with glue and make a collage with fabrics, or scraps of colored and textured papers and cardboard. You could even use needle and thread to stitch a picture - it's up to you! It's fun to be creative.

Paper bank

Recycling makes sense when it comes to making artwork. Envelopes, letters, catalogs, newspapers, and magazines are all useful. And look out for more unusual paper and cardboard: packaging often includes good quality cardboard as well as acetate panels; after a day's outing you may have a pocketful of tickets and maps; save wrappers from candies, and all the crinkly papers from inside a chocolate box; hoard scraps of tissue paper, greaseproof paper, aluminum foil, and corrugated cardboard; and ask friends and family for interesting pieces of fabric and felt.

Crafty tips
You can buy special acrylic paper, available in single sheets or pads, from art shops. This is the best paper to use, as its surface has been specially treated. Or use pieces of cardboard, cut from a cardboard box, and paint it on both sides with a layer of latex paint before you start painting with acrylics.

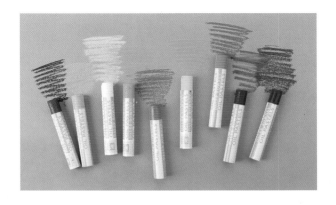

Drawing materials

In your pencil case or tin, keep a few pencils, an eraser and pencil sharpener, a black marker pen, and a fine tipped black felt pen. A ruler is useful, too.

Then a basic set of colored pencils is great for sketching. When birthdays and Christmas come around, you could ask for a wider selection of colored pencils, or maybe some oil pastels, a box of water color paints and some pads of good quality drawing paper.

Use your own money to buy wax crayons. You will also need some sticky tape and glue, for sticking.

Sticking tips

As you experiment with collage, you will find you need different types of glue for sticking different things.

A glue stick is great for all kinds of paper and cardboard. White craft glue will stick bulkier things – even pieces of wood and plastic – but you may need to use quite a lot and leave plenty of time for it to dry. Fabric glue is best for most fabrics, especially thin ones, as it will not soak through or stain – but use it in a very thin layer. Glitter glue is great for sticking sequins and beads, and adds an extra touch of sparkle!

41

Painting with Acrylics

One of the brilliant things you can do with acrylic paints is to blend colors together; another is overpainting one color on top of another, and then there's the thickness of the paint which allows you to build up interesting textures. Try these projects and test the special qualities of acrylics for yourself.

You will need:
acrylic paper or cardboard
acrylic paints
paintbrushes
black paper
scissors
glue stick

Paint a firework picture

This involves blending paints to produce an atmospheric background, with a bit of overpainting to create very effective fireworks.

1 Paint three bands of color – blue, purple, and orange – and brush the edges of each color with a dry brush to blend colors together.

2 When the background is dry, paint starburst fireworks with pale colors such as pink, yellow, and pale blue, using a fine brush, then add dots of white paint.

3 Finally, cut out a skyline of buildings from black paper and, when your painting is dry, stick it in place along the bottom edge, using a glue stick.

How to paint a 3D space rocket picture

This picture is created by overpainting several colors. The rocket is painted separately and flies above the background surface, creating a 3D effect.

You will need:
acrylic paper or cardboard
pencil
ruler
acrylic paints
paintbrushes
glue stick
matchbox

1 With pencil and ruler, draw a rectangle on a sheet of paper or board. This is your picture area. Draw a circle, to represent a planet.

2 Paint the circle pale blue and the background a dark blue – almost black. Leave to dry.

43

3 To make the planet look more realistic, paint patches of blue in different shades to represent sea and land.

4 Paint multicolored stars in the sky. To do this, make a blob of paint and, with the other end of your paintbrush, pull out lines of paint all round.

5 Paint a rocket on a separate sheet of paper or board. When dry, cut it out. Using a glue stick, attach a matchbox to the background and stick the rocket on top.

Geometric Patterns

You don't need any special equipment to produce patterns on paper – these were made with a potato! Ask an adult to help you cut potatoes into shapes and make sure you cover your work surface with plenty of newspaper, as potato printing can be very messy.

Safety tip

It is best to cut the potato with a sharp kitchen knife. Ask an adult to do this for you. A single potato can be used to make several different patterns – just slice off the pattern you have just made, to produce a clean surface, and start again.

You will need:
potatoes
knife (see safety tip)
acrylic paints or poster paints
paintbrush
paper

1 Cut potatoes into simple shapes. Brush the surface with paint, not too thick.

2 Press the painted surface of the potato on to a sheet of paper. Repeat the print in a regular pattern all over the paper.

3 If you like, add a second shape when the first is dry.

Printing a brick wall

Cut a piece of potato into a rectangle. Using several shades of orange and brown paint, brush the surface of the potato with a slightly different mixture of colors each time and print a regular pattern all over a sheet of paper. Why not use the brick pattern as a background for a picture? Or print brick patterns all over a cardboard box, to make a house.

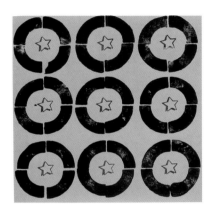

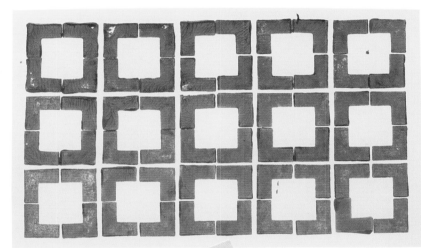

45

Pattern pictures

Repeat a simple shape to make a picture, like this truck. This is a great way to make cards or party invitations as you can print a number of pictures, all the same.

Random Patterns

It can be interesting to make patterns on paper and never know quite how they will turn out. Here are some ideas that are great fun to do, and require very little skill or special materials.

How to make a Wandering marble pattern

With the help of a marble and some thick paint, build up stripes or spiralling circles.

1 Place a sheet of paper in the tray or lid.

2 Dip a marble in paint, place it on the paper and tilt the tray or box lid so the marble rolls, leaving a trail of paint.

3 Produce striped patterns by rolling the marble backward and forward, or scribbly patterns by rolling the marble round and round in circles. Wash the marble, dip it in another color and roll again!

4 Remove the paper and place it on a pad of newspaper or a plastic bag, until dry, and start again with another sheet of paper and different colored paints.

5 When your painted patterns are dry, you can cut them out and assemble them to make pictures or patterns. What about a sea of blue stripes and a swirling orange sun?

You will need:
plastic tray or large cardboard box lid
sheets of thick paper
glass marble
acrylic paints

46

How to paint abstract patterns

When you combine different techniques in one picture, it is called multimedia. Try this: paint a pattern with acrylics, then stick on paper shapes to add an extra dimension. You don't have to copy this pattern – try one of your own!

You will need:
acrylic paper or cardboard
pencil and ruler
acrylic paints
paintbrushes
compasses or round template
newspaper
scissors
PVA glue

1 Divide the paper into eight sections using a pencil and ruler. Paint each section in a shade of yellow. Paint two straight lines in orange, dividing the picture roughly into quarters. Leave to dry.

2 Draw circles in a random pattern all over the picture. Use compasses or draw around a circular object. Paint each circle. Leave to dry.

3 Cut smaller circles from newspaper. Brush white craft glue over the painted circles and stick a newspaper circle on each one. Brush over with more glue: it will be white and semi-opaque at this stage but will be transparent when it dries.

47

Splatter patterns

Dip an old toothbrush in paint and draw a popsicle stick or the blade of a plastic knife across the bristles, causing the paint to splatter over a sheet of paper. Use as many colors as you like to build up patterns. Experiment with various thicknesses of paint to produce different results – and always protect the work surface and floor with plenty of newspapers, as this technique can be very messy!

Printing

The great thing about a print is that you can repeat it and make lots of copies – perfect for invitations or Christmas cards!

Safety tips

The lino cutter is sharp. When cutting lino, always cut away from you. Use your spare hand to hold the edge of the lino that is nearest to you – never put your hand in front of the cutting tool, in case it slips. Protect your work surface with plenty of newspaper.

How to print a lino cut horse

You will need:
lino
light-colored pencil
lino-cutting tool
water-based lino printing ink
sheet of plastic
roller
paper

This technique requires a special lino-cutting tool, a piece of special lino, a small roller, and some printing ink, all of which are available from art and craft shops.

If you are a newcomer to this craft, start by buying a handle and just two cutters: a pointed v-shaped one for cutting fine lines and details, and a scoop-shaped one for cutting away larger areas.

1 Draw a picture on the surface of the lino, using a light-colored pencil. Remember that, whatever design you draw, it will be reversed when you print it.

2 Cut away the parts of the design that you do not wish to print. The areas that you cut away will not be covered with ink and so the paper will show through.

48

3 Squeeze out a little ink on to a sheet of plastic. You can use a piece of acetate, or a plastic bag stretched out and attached to your work surface round all edges with masking tape. Roll out the ink until the roller is evenly covered, then roll it across the surface of the lino until it is covered with a thin film of ink.

4 Place a sheet of paper on top of the lino and rub gently all over, to press the ink on to the paper. Carefully peel away the paper and leave to dry.

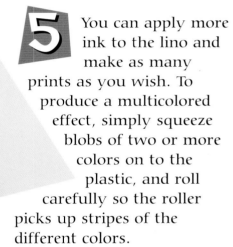

5 You can apply more ink to the lino and make as many prints as you wish. To produce a multicolored effect, simply squeeze blobs of two or more colors on to the plastic, and roll carefully so the roller picks up stripes of the different colors.

49

Leaf prints

Coat leaves with paint, using a brush or roller, then press on to paper. Different leaves will give different results – try choosing ones with prominent veins. Print an all-over pattern of leaves or cut out individual leaf prints to make greetings cards or gift tags.

Wax Crayons

Crayons are not just for little kids. Their waxy texture makes them perfect for all kinds of special techniques, from rubbings to wax resist! Try some of these...

You will need:
large sheets of paper
dark-colored, chunky
wax crayons

How to make a brass rubbing

Objects with a raised texture can be used to make interesting pictures. You place a sheet of paper on top, rub all over with a crayon and the patterns are reproduced as if by magic! Brass plaques can be found in some churches or museums and are ideal for rubbings. You may have to ask permission before you start – and be careful not to mark or damage the precious brasses!

1 Place the paper over the brass plaque. You can weight down the corners of a large sheet with pebbles or other heavy objects.

2 Making sure the paper doesn't slip as you work, rub all over the surface, above the brass, using the side of the crayon. Start gently, making light marks, and build up until the picture becomes darker.

Wax butterfly

Shave wax crayons using a chunky pencil sharpener. Arrange the shavings in a pattern on one side of a folded sheet of paper. Fold the paper to enclose the shavings, place inside a sheet of newspaper, and press with a hot iron – with the assistance of an adult. When you open out the paper, you will have a symmetrical pattern of melted wax.

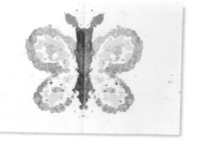

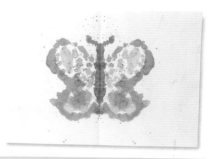

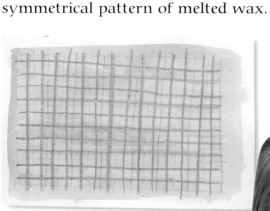

51

Magic pictures

Wax and water do not mix. Make a drawing on a sheet of paper using a wax crayon. Brush over it with water color paint. Instead of a crayon, try using a candle – a white candle on white paper produces a "magic" result!

Making Maps

Maps have fascinated artists for centuries. Here are two ideas for you to try. Make your own ancient treasure map, or use a tourist map as the base for a colorful souvenir collage.

You will need:
large sheet of cartridge paper
pencil
brown water color paint or ink
pen holder and nib, or
brown felt tip pen
colored pencils
beeswax polish
kitchen towels or old rags
length of ribbon or string

Make a pirate treasure map

With a couple of simple techniques, you can transform a humble sheet of white cartridge paper into ancient parchment!

1 Start by drawing the basic shape of your treasure island in pencil.

2 Dilute brown water color paint or ink and rub all over the paper, using a piece of kitchen towel or old rag.

52

3 With pen and ink, or felt tip pen, outline the island and draw in details such as arrows to show sea currents, trees, and mountains. Use colored pencils to add a touch of faded color.

4 Dip a kitchen towel or rag into wax polish and rub all over the paper, front and back. This should soak in and make the paper slightly translucent and leathery.

5 Fold and refold the paper until it has thick creases in it. Try rubbing a finger dipped in brown paint or ink along the creases. Crumple the paper and smooth it out again. Tear the edges of the paper and tear along some of the creases. Roll up the corners.

6 Finally, fold up the map and tie a scrap of ribbon or string around it.

53

Vacation Souvenir

The next time you go on vacation – or even out on a day trip – save brochures, leaflets, bus tickets, and so on. Stick a map of the place you have visited on a sheet of cardboard, then glue the other paraphernalia on top to make a special collage to remind you of your trip!

Notebooks

Artists like to carry a notebook with them so they can make sketches and jot down ideas. And a portfolio is useful, too – a kind of folder to keep your best drawings safe. Why not make your own? Just find some scrap paper and cardboard, and follow the instructions carefully.

How to make a heart-throb notebook

You can use this book for little sketches – or you may prefer to stick in pictures of your favorite actors or pop stars instead!

You will need:
3 sheets of red paper about 10 x 8 inches
scrap cardboard
scissors
pencil
needle and thread

54

1 Cut a heart-shaped template from scrap cardboard.

2 Fold a sheet of red paper in quarters and place the template on top, with one edge on the fold on one of the longer sides. Draw around the template and cut out, to produce two double hearts with the fold running up the center. Repeat with the other two sheets of red paper.

3 You now have six double hearts. Open them out and place them all in a pile. With needle and thread, stitch through the folds, through all layers. Knot the ends of the thread firmly. Decorate the cover.

Shirt notebook

You can make a notebook in almost any shape. You can use more pages than for the heart-throb notepad. Why not personalize this notebook by using your own choice of colors and patterns? You could make a T-shirt design instead, or even a copy of your favorite shirt!

How to make a portfolio

Here is the perfect way to keep a collection of your drawings flat and dust-free!

You will need:
2 sheets of cardboard
wrapping paper or decorative
self-adhesive paper
carpet tape
2 sheets of
colored paper
glue stick
ribbon

55

1 Cut wrapping paper or self-adhesive paper about 1 inch larger all round than the cardboard. Stick these to one side of each piece of cardboard, folding the excess to the other side.

2 Place the two covered cardboard pieces, wrong side upward, about $1/2$ inch apart, to form the front and back covers. Cut a length of carpet tape just over twice the height of the cardboard and use it to bridge the gap between the two covers, forming a spine.

3 Make two slits, one in each of the covers, in the center, near the open edges. Push a length of ribbon through each and stick the end in place on the inside.

4 Trim a little from the two sheets of colored paper and, using the glue stick, stick these inside the covers, hiding the edges of the cover paper and the ribbons.

Fabric and Thread

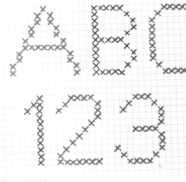

It was a tradition in the nineteenth century for young children to learn cross stitch. They would practice their skills by making samplers, consisting of rows of alphabet letters and simple pictures, and the cross stitch letters would also be sewn onto clothes and bed sheets, as an identifying mark.

Simple as ABC

Start with this simple sampler, to practice the stitch technique.

You will need:
graph paper
colored felt tip pens
cross stitch fabric
embroidery hoop
tapestry needle
embroidery floss
scissors

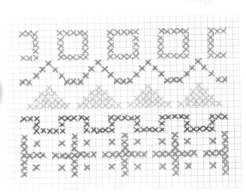

1 Draw out your design on graph paper. Fill in one square with a cross to represent each stitch. You can copy the one from this page or make up your own.

2 Stretch your fabric in an embroidery hoop. Thread your needle with three strands of floss. At the back of the fabric, run the needle under a few rows of the fabric weave, to hold the end of the floss in place.

3 Bring the needle through one of the holes to the front of the fabric. To make a single cross stitch, push the needle through the hole diagonally opposite the one it has come up through. Then make a second diagonal stitch that crosses over the first.

4 Follow the design you have drawn, making a series of cross stitches to correspond with the ones on the graph.

5 When you have finished stitching, remove the fabric from the hoop, and trim it to the size and shape you want. Fray the edges by pulling out some of the threads.

Pattern picture

Have fun designing rows of patterns on your graph paper then translating these patterns onto stitches. Zigzags are easy, so are crosses and squares. By practising your stitches in this way, you will be able to produce a colorful and attractive picture. Stitch a border all around to make it complete.

57

Cross stitch materials
Cross stitch fabric is specially woven to create a grid pattern with holes through which to push your needle and create neat stitches in the form of a cross. The fabric can be finely or coarsely woven. If you are a beginner, choose a coarse fabric, with 10 or 12 holes to 2.5cm of fabric. The sales assistant in the store will help you.
The needle to use is a tapestry needle, which has a slightly blunt point. Embroidery floss is made up of six strands. Cut a length of floss, then pull out three individual strands, and thread these into your needle.

Potted plants

As you become more confident, try designing pictures instead of letters and patterns. It is slightly more challenging but great fun. You could try to copy this picture onto graph paper, or make up one of your own.

Fabric Pictures

One of the best things about making pictures with fabrics is the wide variety of colors, textures, and thicknesses available. Collect together as many different scraps as you can: they could be from old clothes you were otherwise going to throw away, or pieces from friends who like to sew.

Fabric picture

Stitching fabric pieces on to a fabric background is known as appliqué. Keep shapes simple and use a variety of colored fabric scraps to produce a charming, country-style picture!

You will need:
small pieces of fabric
larger piece of fabric, for background
pins
needle and thread
scissors

1   Cut out a variety of shapes from fabrics. Pin them in place on the background fabric.

2   To stitch them in place, fold under the edge and stitch the fold to the background fabric. This is fiddly but quite easy. Make your stitches as small as possible, for a neat finish.

3   Turn under the edges of the background fabric, to neaten them. You can glue the fabric picture to a piece of thick cardboard, to display it if you wish.

Make a felt picture

Felt is great
for making
all sorts of
things and
inexpensive
to buy. Cut
scraps into
shapes, keep
them in a box,
then take them
out and make pictures.
When you have
finished playing, they
can go back in the box
ready for another day!

1 Cover the
box with
fabric. Glue
a piece of felt inside
the lid, to use as a
background for
your pictures.

You will need:
box with a lid
large and small
pieces of felt
scissors
glue

2 Cut shapes from felt. Geometric
shapes such as squares and
triangles are useful for
constructing buildings. Circles and
strips can be made into trees and people.
Use your imagination!

Tissue Paper

Tissue paper is fragile and semi-transparent; it can be cut, torn, crumpled, and layered – so make use of these unique properties to create some special pictures!

Stained glass

This type of picture looks best displayed with light shining through it – so tape your finished artwork to a window or prop it on a windowsill, for the best effect.

You will need:
thin black cardboard
colored tissue paper
sticky tape or glue stick
scissors

1 Draw a simple design on the black cardboard. Using scissors, cut out areas you wish to appear in color.

2 Trace through the holes you have cut on to pieces of colored tissue. Cut out these shapes, adding a bit all round, for sticking.

3 Stick the tissue paper pieces to the reverse side of the black cut-out, using glue stick or sticky tape.

Tissue paper cutouts

Being very thin, tissue paper is extremely easy to fold and you can cut through several layers at once. Try folding and cutting to produce shapes or motifs. Stick to simple shapes until you have had a bit of practice. Then stick your cutouts on to a sheet of paper of a contrasting color.

Paper pellet picture

Use small pieces of tissue paper, screwed up into balls, to add texture to a picture. Draw or paint a picture first, or use colored paper cutouts. You could add tissue paper pellets to make flowers, or to add texture to hair on a portrait.

Portraits

If you want to be a serious artist, you will probably want to try your hand at portraiture! But if you can't get anyone to sit still for long enough, don't despair – just use photographs, like other artists do!

Colored pencil portrait

Colored pencils are a good medium to start with as they are inexpensive, easy to use, and you can build up your drawing slowly until you are pleased with the result.

You will need:
sheet of good quality
cartridge paper
pencil, preferably 4B
colored pencils (see tip below)
photograph for reference

Colored pencils
You do not need many colors to start with. A basic set of 12 colored pencils is a good starting point, as colors can be mixed on the paper. You may like to try soluble pencils, which are exactly like ordinary colored pencils with the added bonus that, if you go over your pencil lines with a paintbrush dipped in water, the color dissolves so it looks like water color paint!

Pencil portrait

Start with a simple portrait in pencil. Choose good quality cartridge paper, which has a slightly rough, textured surface, and a pencil with a fairly soft lead, such as a 4B. Draw a grid of guidelines on your paper and lay an acetate grid over the photo you wish to copy. Carefully copy the shapes within each square on to the larger squares on your paper. Rub out the grid lines, then add detail.

1 Scale up the photograph to the size you want, using the simple method described below.

2 Once you have sketched the outline of your subject, using pencil, use colored pencils to add color and shading. It will not matter if you have not got exactly the right shade of colored pencil as colors can be mixed. Practice on a scrap of paper, starting with a light color, shading very gently, then going over this with other colors, again very gently, until you have built up the shade you want.

3 Keep referring to your photograph. You do not have to reproduce every detail – this is your picture and you can change whatever you like and leave things out, if you wish!

63

Mosaic Magic

By cutting out and sticking down pieces of colored paper to make pictures and patterns, you can create some very bold, colorful effects. And you don't have to go out and buy colored paper – use pages from catalogs and magazines, and scraps of wrapping paper.

Clown with rainbow border

You will need:
sheet of colored paper
pencil
ruler
small scraps of colored paper
scissors
glue stick

1 Draw a line, a ruler's width, all round the paper, to form a border.

2 Cut colored paper into thin strips and glue these down to fill the border area with a striped, colorful pattern.

3 Cut shapes from colored paper to make the clown's head, body, legs, and so on. Arrange these in the center of the background, sticking each piece neatly in place.

Mermaid with shiny rainbow border

As well as plain colored papers, look for shiny, metallic papers. Cut these into strips and make a border, as before. To make the mermaid's tail sparkle and shimmer, glue on masses of sequins, using glitter glue.

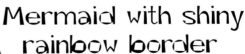

How to make a cheerful cockerel collage

Start with a large sheet of thick cardboard, as a base, and stick on a sheet of slightly smaller colored paper, to form a background. Cut out shapes from different colored papers – a body, head, feet, wing, and so on – and stick these in place using a glue stick.

Add a border of mosaic squares and, because this is the most colorful occupant in the hen house, why not add some bright cutout starbursts of colored paper as a final flourish?

Textured Collage

Building up a picture or patterns by sticking things on to a background is called "collage." You can use all kinds of things – paper, plastic, fabric – and here are some ideas to get you started.

You will need:
silver card
black corrugated paper, 12 x 8 inches
scraps of colored corrugated paper
holographic paper
sequins, round stickers scissors,
glue stick etc.

How to make a robot collage

Metallic cardboard and paper is great for making really shiny collages. Scraps of corrugated paper add interesting texture. Follow the basic instructions but use your own imagination, as well as any interesting scraps you have to hand, to create your very own customized robot.

66

1 From silver card, cut rectangles of assorted sizes. Arrange these to form the robot's head, body, arms, and legs. When you are satisfied with your arrangement, stick the pieces in place on the black corrugated paper background.

2 Cut out shapes from corrugated paper and holographic paper to make hands, boots, and so on. Stick these in place.

3 Finally, add details such as nuts, bolts, and dials with stickers, sequins, and scraps such as a barcode cut from a magazine or packaging.

How to make a pizza picture

You will need:
plain and corrugated colored paper
glue stick
sheet of light-colored card,
approximately 14 x 12 inches
scissors

1 Start with the background. Cut 3/4 inch squares of blue paper and stick down to form a checkerboard pattern, giving the impression of a tablecloth.

2 Cut a circle of brown corrugated paper and a slightly smaller circle of plain beige paper, to form the pizza base. Stick in place.

3 Cut out a big splat from red paper, to suggest tomato sauce, and triangles of yellow paper for cheese. Cut circles of pink corrugated paper for pepperoni, mushroom shapes from beige corrugated paper, and small pieces of green paper for chunks of green capsicum. Stick everything in place.

67

4 As a final touch, cut out knife and fork shapes from gray or silver paper – or photographs of real flatware from a magazine or catalog.

Rainbow tree

Draw a tree with lots of bare branches on a sheet of beige or brown paper. Cut this out and stick, using a glue stick, to a sheet of thin card, or thick paper. Cut leaf shapes from plain and patterned paper. Look for patches of color and pattern in a magazine or catalog. Stick the leaves all around the tree.

Papercraft

Paper is marvelous stuff! It comes in all kinds of colors and textures, matt or shiny, plain or patterned. Save scraps of paper from other projects, and cut pieces from magazines and catalogs. Keep all your scraps in a box, so you'll have a wide variety to choose from when you want to make a picture.

Coat rack

Customize this design with representations of your own coat and bag, to make a really personal picture.

You will need:
cardboard or thick paper, for background
plain and patterned paper scraps
scissors
glue stick

1 Start by cutting a strip of brown paper to represent the coat rack. Cut a second, smaller strip and stick it on top to make it appear more three-dimensional. Cut circles of paper to represent pegs.

2 Now cut shapes from various colored and patterned papers, for clothes. Cut a hanger from silver paper, for example, and, to make a pair of pants to go over the hanger, crease the paper to look like folded fabric.

Trash can

To make this picture look really three-dimensional, cover a shallow box with gray paper, for the trash can, then fill with all kinds of bits and pieces such as crumpled candy wrappers. Make flies from cut-out paper shapes, drawing wiggly flight paths with pen or pencil. Have fun and let your imagination run away with you!

Tile designs

Start with a square of cardboard and play around with colors and shapes: a central star, triangles, squares, and dots. When you have stuck down all the pieces, protect the surface by covering with clear self-adhesive film, or by brushing with diluted white craft glue to give a glossy finish.

Cards and Gifts

contents

71

Introduction

A home-made gift or greeting is not only more special than one you can buy in the stores – it's also likely to be a lot cheaper. With paper and scissors, or fabric and thread, or cardboard, glue, and paint, you can make gifts for moms, dads, aunties, babies, friends, teachers – for any person and any occasion!

Whether it's a birthday, an anniversary, a wedding, or the birth of a baby, there are plenty of ideas in *Cards and Gifts* to inspire you to make something extra special.

For a quick and easy present, a bookmark or set of personalized stationery can be put together with just some scraps of colored paper, scissors, and a glue stick!

Fabric or paper?

If you want to try your hand at sewing, there are lots of things to make. Choose your fabrics carefully, though. Something that will need a lot of washing should be made from a cotton fabric, which means you will have to neaten raw edges and sew things together firmly so they don't come apart! Felt is easier to stitch but not washable – so it's not suitable for aprons, towels, babies' bibs, or anything that will need laundering! You can make some great gifts from papier mâché – but remember to plan ahead. Paper and glue need time to dry, and painting and varnishing can take longer than you think, so remember to take this into consideration!

Ribbons, tapes, and trimmings

Ribbon is good for tying things! Collect as many different kinds as you can. They can be made from thin, transparent fabrics, satin, velvet, or even paper. Try to gather together different colors and widths. Ribbon is cheaper to buy in markets than in craft stores.

Crafty tips
To bind the edge of fabric with bias binding, open up the binding and place one edge level with the raw edge of the fabric. Stitch along the fold, through both thicknesses of fabric. Then fold the binding over the edge of the fabric and, on the other side, stitch down the other folded edge, using neat stitches.

Bias binding is a special kind of folded tape, usually made from cotton, that is extremely useful in sewing projects for covering the raw edges of fabric. Used to edge a baby's bib, or a cushion cover, it also provides a nice, colorful border (see box for tips on how to sew).

While you're on the lookout for things to collect together for your work box, save buttons, snap fastenings, zippers, lengths of cord, different kinds of threads, pins (glass-headed ones are best, as you can see them easily), and needles of various sizes. Scissors, a tape measure, string, paper, paints and brushes, fabric glue and glitter will also come in useful.

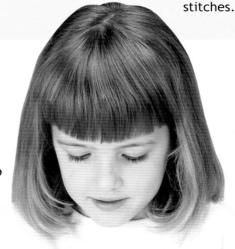

Say it with Flowers

Whatever the occasion, flowers are a good choice for greetings cards. Here are some simple but very eye-catching ideas.

3D flower card

Simple paper cutouts can be given an extra dimension by folding and adding a real ribbon bow to tie up the bouquet!

You will need:
small sheet of thin colored cardboard
scraps of colored paper
glue stick
small, round stickers
short lengths of ribbon and string
scissors

2 Cut out six-petaled flower shapes from white and yellow cardboard. Pinch each petal between your finger and thumb then, applying a blob of glue to the center of each flower, stick them in place. Add a small sticker to each flower center.

3 Make two holes, one either side of the flower stems, thread ribbon through, and tie in a bow.

1 Fold the card in half. Cut green paper into thin strips and glue in place, to make stems.

4 Finally, cut a label from a scrap of paper, add a sticker, and punch a hole, threading it with string.

Chunky flower cards

Cut simple shapes from thick cardboard – flower pots, stems, leaves, and flowers – and paint the front and edges of each piece. When the paint is dry, stick the pieces on the front of a folded card for a really good 3D effect.

Gift Wrapping

Have you got an awkward-shaped gift to wrap? A jar, perhaps, a key ring, or even a banana-shaped pen? Here are some bright ideas!

Gift bag

It is easier than you may think to produce a very impressive result. Just follow the steps below.

You will need:
small rectangular box
thick wrapping paper
double-sided sticky tape
hole punch
ribbon
scissors

1 Cut a piece of wrapping paper wide enough to go around the box with a $^1/_2$in overlap, and about $1^1/_4$in–$1^1/_2$in longer at either end.

2 Wrap the paper around the box and stick the edges together using double-sided tape.

3 At one end of the box, neatly fold in the edges and stick down using double-sided tape, to form the base of the bag.

4 Remove the box. Neaten the top edge by folding it inside, or simply cut it off to the desired height.

5 Make two holes at the front and back, about $^1/_2$in from the top, and thread with ribbon, knotting it on the inside to form handles.

Tissue paper straw

Roll up a sheet of tissue paper and flatten it. Cut across into very thin strips. Gather the strips in your hands and crumple slightly, then fluff them out.

Cardboard tube

Save tubes from toilet rolls or kitchen paper! Slip the gift inside, then cut a piece of wrapping paper twice the length of the tube and wide enough to go around it with a $^1/_2$in overlap. Wrap the paper around the tube and glue or tape in place. At one end, neatly fold over the paper, then cut a circle of paper and glue in place for a neat finish. At the other end, gather the paper and tie with a length of ribbon after putting the gift inside.

Pyramid

Cut a square of cardboard to form the base, then draw four triangles with the same measurement as the square for their base. Apply glue to one side of each piece and place them flat on a piece of wrapping paper with the square in the center and one triangle on each side. Cut out the paper, about $^1/_2$in all round. Fold the paper over and stick in place. Cover with pieces of paper, cut to shape, in a contrasting color. Punch a hole on the point of each triangle, thread with ribbon, pop a present inside, and tie closed.

Baby Gifts

WARNING
Always ask an adult to check that the toy you have made is safe to give to a baby or small child. Remember to ensure there are no buttons or other small items which could cause choking.

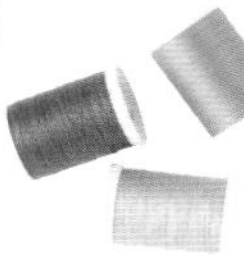

The birth of a baby is always a great occasion. Celebrate by making one of these gifts – very easy even if you are a beginner at sewing – or a card with the baby's name.

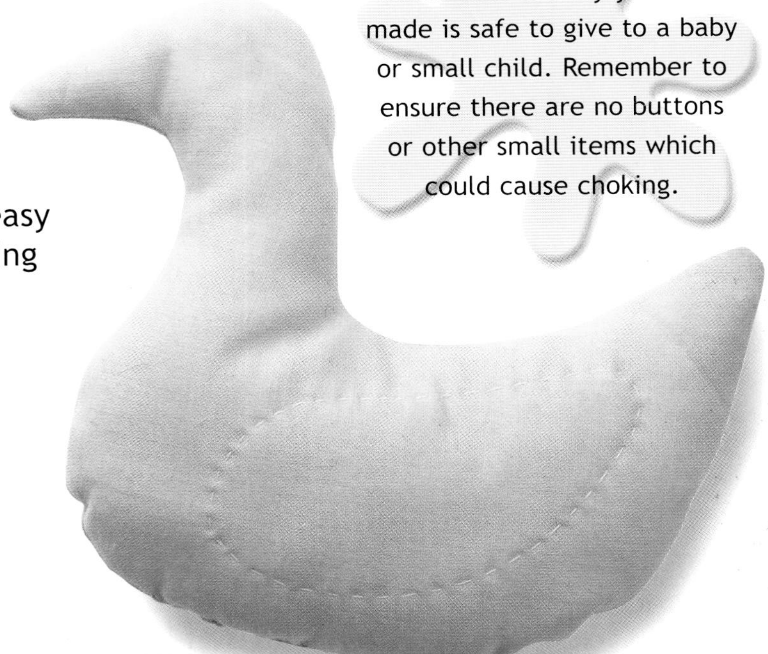

Flat duck

You will need:
pieces of cotton fabric
needle and thread
polyester stuffing

Cut two identical duck shapes from cotton fabric. Put the two shapes together with the right side of the fabric on the inside. Stitch all round, leaving a small gap so you can turn your duck inside out. Push stuffing through the gap, then neatly sew the gap closed.

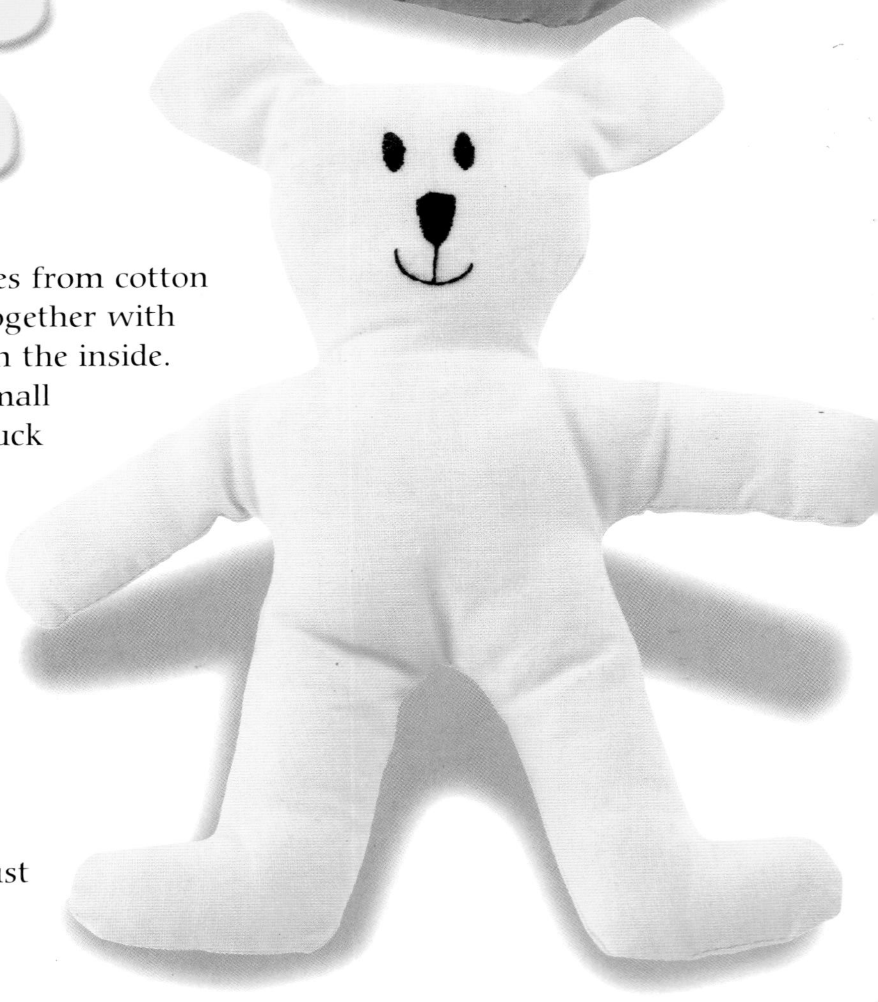

Teddy

This teddy is made, just like the duck from two fabric shapes stitched together and stuffed. Make three bears, just like in the story, or make other animal shapes.

Teddy card

Fold a long strip of thin cardboard in accordion folds. The number of folds will depend on the number of letters in the baby's name. Draw a teddy shape on the top of the folded cardboard, making sure the arms and legs go over the folds. Cut through all layers and open out the card. You should have a row of teddies, joined together by their paws. Decorate with eyes, noses, and letters cut from colored paper.

Presents for Pets

Even pets can get presents! Doesn't your favorite animal deserve a special treat?

Painted pet bowls

Using special paints suitable for decorating china, paint your design – such as a fish bone for a cat – leave it to dry and, following the manufacturer's instructions, ask an adult to bake the dish in a hot oven to set the paint.

Felt mouse

Cut a heart shape from felt, fold in half, and stitch all round, leaving a small gap for stuffing. You can stuff it with sawdust or absorbent cotton, then sew up the opening. Add circles of felt for ears, sewn firmly in place, beady eyes, and a tail of plaited yarn with a bell on the end.

Pet place mats

Plastic-coated mats are a practical idea as they can be wiped clean – perfect if your cat or dog is a messy eater!

You will need:
sheet of colored cardboard
scraps of colored paper
glue stick
clear self-adhesive film

1 Cut a basic cat or dog shape from paper, stick it in place on the sheet of cardboard, then add details, also cut from colored paper.

2 When you are happy with your design, cover both back and front with clear adhesive film.

81

Crafty tips
Instead of covering your finished picture with self-adhesive film, you could have it laminated. Some photocopy stores or office suppliers offer this service and it gives a really hard-wearing, long-lasting result.

Gifts for Busy People

Grown-ups lead such busy lives! Here are some clever gift ideas to help them to get organized!

Key rings

You can make one key ring – or one each for the keys to the house, car, and office, or whatever is appropriate! You can buy split rings from a craft store, stationers or shoe repairers.

You will need:
scraps of cardboard
paperclips
tissue paper
white craft glue
paints
split rings

1 Cut circles of cardboard and stick two together, with half a paperclip sandwiched in the middle, poking out to form a small hook.

2 Dilute the craft glue with water, about two parts glue to one part water, and brush it over both sides of the cardboard, covering with strips of tissue paper. Build up about three or four layers. Hang up to dry.

3 Paint a design on the disc – a car for car keys, a house for house keys, and so on.

4 Clip the split ring on to the paperclip hook.

Fur fabric purse

It's very easy to make a simple purse. Just cut a rectangle of fabric and stitch the two shorter ends to either side of a short zipper. Then, with the fabric inside out, stitch up the two sides. Fur fabric is ideal, as any untidy stitching will be hidden by the thick fur pile. You can stick goggle eyes on if you wish.

Memo pad

Stick paper shapes to a rectangle of colored cardboard, and stick a small note pad in the center. If you want to fix the pad to the refrigerator, stick a strip of magnetic tape, available from craft stores, to the back of the cardboard. Or you could make two small holes, thread with string or ribbon so that the pad can be hung up.

Stationery Set

Even in the e-mail age, some people like to send old-fashioned letters – and a trio of boxes to hold stationery, letters, and stamps would make a fantastic present!

You will need:
thick cardboard
ruler
pencil
scissors
white craft glue
newspaper
paints
paintbrushes

Letter rack

The basic shape is simple to construct from pieces of cardboard and is covered with papier mâché to make it really strong and hard-wearing.

1 Cut four rectangles of thick cardboard, measuring 9in x 4$\frac{1}{2}$in (for the base) and 8$\frac{1}{2}$in x 7in, 8$\frac{1}{4}$in x 5in, and 8$\frac{1}{2}$in x 3in, for the dividers. Glue the dividers to the base, using the finished letter rack, pictured below, as a guide.

8$\frac{1}{2}$in

8$\frac{1}{4}$in

7in

5in

3in

4$\frac{1}{2}$in

2 Then stand the construction on its side, on a piece of cardboard, and draw around it to give you the shape needed for the two sides. Cut these out and stick in place.

3 Dilute the craft glue, 2 parts glue to one part water, and brush it all over the construction, covering with three layers of torn newspaper strips. Leave to dry.

4 Paint the letter rack, inside and out, adding your choice of decoration. Simple flowers and spots are easy to do and very effective!

Stationery box

Paint a box lid inside and out, decorating it with painted flowers or other motifs. Why not paint it with a similar pattern to the letter rack, to make a matching set? Cut paper to fit, stamping it with the person's initials, if you wish, or with a decorative stamp.

Stamp box

Cover a small cardboard or wooden box with postage stamps. To remove used stamps from envelopes, tear the envelope, leaving a small margin of paper all round the stamp, and soak in a bowl of water until the stamp floats free of the paper. Dry on kitchen paper, then glue to the box using craft glue diluted with water. Once you have covered the box with stamps, you may wish to varnish it, to make the surface more hard-wearing.

Desk Tidies

Most grown-ups would find these items very useful, on their office desk, or even in the kitchen to keep paper, envelopes and a pen or pencil always to hand! There's even a bookmark to mark a page in the diary!

Stationery folder

Not only is this a nice present for someone – but it should encourage them to write you a thank-you letter!

You will need:
sheet of cardboard about 10in x 8in
scraps of colored paper
glue stick
sticky tape
ribbon
stamp or stencil, for decorating envelopes

1 Fold the cardboard in half, then fold in ³/₄in at either side and 1¹/₄in along the bottom. Cut away the corners along the fold lines, then glue the folded-in edges together at the two bottom corners.

2 Cut slits, one on each side, and insert a piece of ribbon into each, securing the ends with a small piece of sticky tape, hidden under the folds.

3 Cut pieces of paper, each 6¹/₂in x4¹/₂in, decorating each one with the recipient's name, or a small motif, or both.

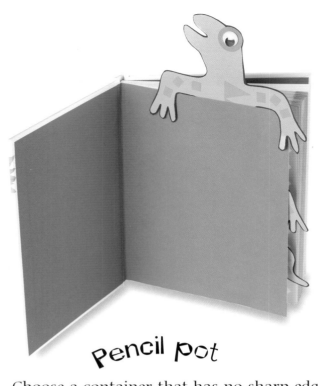

Lizard bookmark

Cut a lizard shape from green paper, stick it to black cardboard and cut around the outline again. Add scales cut from paler green paper, and a beady eye! The lizard's front legs slip over the front of the page!

Pencil pot

Choose a container that has no sharp edges. A cocoa or custard powder tin is ideal. Cover the outside with a strips of paper, then cut pencil shapes from colored paper and stick all round, using a glue stick.

Family Photo Fun

Relatives will love a present with a picture of their favorite grandchild or nephew or niece or other family member. To avoid damaging precious photographic prints, have photocopies made. Black and white ones are cheaper than color – and very eye-catching!

Photo calendar

Inexpensive calendars – just the days and dates, without any pictures – are available from stationers very cheaply, or you could print out your own, with the help of a computer.

You will need:
empty CD case
small calendar
colored paper
photocopies of favorite photos
glue stick

1 Cut twelve pieces of colored paper to fit inside the CD case.

2 Trim photocopies so they are smaller than the colored paper. Stick one in place on each of the pieces of paper and stick on one calendar month below.

OCTOBER
M T W T F S S
1 2 3 4 5 6 7
8 9 10 11 12 13 14
15 16 17 18 19 20 21
22 23 24 25 26 27 28
29 30 31

Photo box

Paint a small wooden or cardboard box – from a craft store or junk store, perhaps. It looks particularly effective if you paint the box all over in one color, such as yellow, then, when this is dry, paint a different color, such as turquoise blue, on top. When dry, lightly rub with sandpaper to reveal some of the color beneath. Stick a favorite photograph on the lid and fill the box with small photos cut to fit.

Photo cube

Cut six equal-sized squares of thin cardboard and join them together with sticky tape, to make a cube. Don't worry if the tape looks untidy – it will be covered up by the pictures! Cut photographs (or photocopies) into squares, the same size as the sides of the cube, and glue in place using a glue stick.

Photo card

Spare photocopies can simply be stuck onto a piece of folded cardboard for a very personal greetings card, suitable for almost any occasion!

Tea Time Treats

The chances are you know someone who really loves a cup of tea or coffee! Here is just the right greetings card for them, and a table mat to stand their cup on! And anyone who enjoys cooking would welcome a home-made pot holder.

Coasters

These colorful table mats are just the right size for a cup or glass – but if you are patient and have the time, you could make larger ones.

You will need:
1 yard cord or thick string
scraps of fabric
embroidery floss
needle
scissors

1 Tear the fabric into strips, 1¼in wide. Place one end of the cord along a strip of fabric, wrap the fabric round, and bind with floss. You do not have to be very neat or even.

2 When you come to the end of the fabric strip, add another strip and carry on binding it with thread. From time to time, tie off the end of one piece of thread and start again with a different color.

3 When you have wrapped the entire length of cord, start coiling it into a tight spiral. Thread your needle with one strand of floss and stitch the edges of the bound cord together as you coil it.

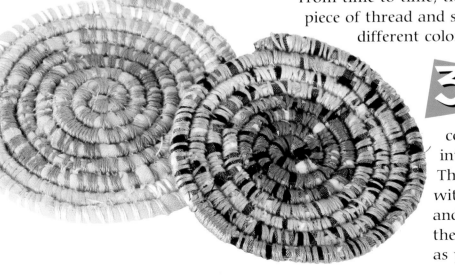

Pot holder

This can be used to hold a hot pot handle or to stand a hot pan on, like a table mat. The layer of batting inside acts as insulation.

You will need:
scraps of plain and patterned cotton fabric
needle and thread
polyester batting
bias binding
button
scissors

1 Cut nine 4in squares from different colored fabrics. Stitch them together.

2 Cut petal shapes from fabric scraps, pin and stitch in place in the center of the patchwork. To do this, simply tuck under the raw edges of the fabric and sew to the background, using tiny stitches.

3 Cut a piece of polyester batting and a piece of backing fabric the same size as your patchwork. Place the backing fabric with the batting on top and the patchwork on top of the other two and stitch together all round, close to the edges.

4 Then bind the edges with bias binding (see introduction). Add a loop of binding for hanging, and a button for decoration.

Tea pot card

Whoever you send this to can have a greetings card and a real cup of tea!

EARL GREY

91

Fold a piece of cardboard in half. On the front, cut out and stick down teapot and teacup shapes. Make a slit below the lid of the teapot and slip the string from a teabag through it. Tape the string inside the front of the card, to keep the teabag in place.

Winter Warmers

B asic sewing and knitting skills are all you need to complete these colorful projects. If you have never picked up a pair of knitting needles or a needle and thread, maybe now is the time to try?

Hot water bottle cover

Vary the motif according to who it is for – a grandparent, a young child, perhaps, or even your dog! You could even use a different colored fleece for each side of the cover.

You will need:
hot water bottle
fleece fabric, about 24in x 16in
scrap paper
pen or pencil
scraps of fabric
needle and thread
ribbon, about 20in
scissors

1 Place a hot water bottle on a piece of paper and draw around it, to make a template slightly larger than the bottle itself. Do not draw around the shape of the neck, but continue the sides up in a straight line. You should end up with a sort of rectangle with two rounded corners.

2 Place the paper template on a double thickness of fleece, pin it in place, and cut out.

3 Decorate one of the fleece shapes with fabric cutouts. See the baby bibs on "Baby Gifts" pages for how to do this.

4 With the right sides facing inward, stitch the two shapes together, about $1/2$in from the edges all round, leaving the top edge open. Turn right sides out.

5 Stitch two lengths of ribbon to the seams, near the top of the cover. Slip the hot water bottle inside, gather the fabric round the top and tie in place.

Cushion

Follow the instructions given and you should create a cushion measuring $8^{1}/2$in square. Feel free to vary the colors and the widths of the stripes, or to make a larger or smaller cushion simply by casting on more or fewer stitches!

You will need:
1oz double knitting yarn in each of 8 colors
number 6 needles
$8^{1}/2$in square pillow (see note)
tapestry needle
scraps of cardboard
scissors

Note
If you don't have a pillow the right size, make one from two squares of fabric stuffed with polyester batting.

93

1 Cast on 80 stitches in your first color (red), then knit 10 rows of plain knitting.

2 Break off the yarn, leaving an end about 8in long, then continue knitting with your second color (orange) and knit 10 rows.

3 Break off the yarn and continue with your third color (yellow). Continue in this way, knitting 10 rows of each color, until you have completed eight stripes and your piece of knitting is $8^{1}/2$in deep. Bind off.

4 Thread the tapestry needle with one of the loose ends of yarn. Fold the knitting in half and stitch the edges together along two sides. Use the correct color of yarn to stitch each stripe, for a neat effect. Push the pillow in through the open side, then stitch this side closed.

5 Make pom poms to decorate the corners. Draw two $2^{1}/2$in circles on a piece of cardboard, and a $1^{1}/4$in circle in the center of each. Cut them out. Place these cardboard rings together and wind round and round with yarn. When the rings are covered with a thick layer of yarn, cut the yarn between the outer edges of the rings, slip a length of yarn between the two rings, and tie tightly, Slip the rings off, then trim the woolly ball with scissors, to neaten it. Stitch in place.

Needlework

If you know someone who likes to sew, they will welcome one of these home-made gifts. Or, if you are keen on sewing, make one for yourself!

Pin cushion

This is easy to make – just find a suitable lid from an old jar and a scrap of colorful fabric.

You will need:
plastic lid, about 3in in diameter
scrap of cotton fabric
needle and thread
polyester batting
fabric glue
pins

1 Cut a circle of fabric about 7in in diameter.

2 Stitch all around the edge of the fabric with a running stitch. Pull the end of the thread to gather the fabric.

3 Place a generous handful of batting in the center of the circle, pull up the thread end tightly, and fasten firmly.

4 Apply glue to the inside of the lid, over the base, and up the sides. Press the fabric ball into the lid and leave until the glue is dry. Stick in some pins.

Felt needle case

Anyone who is keen on needlework –
or has a name tag to stitch or a
button to sew on – will find this
needle case useful.

1 Cut a piece of fabric
8in x 6in. Cut shapes
from felt and stitch
to the right-hand half of
the fabric. This will form
the front cover of the
needle case.

2 Cut two
pieces of
cardboard, each
measuring 4in x 3in and
place them, side by side, on
the wrong side of the fabric,
with a small gap in the
center. Fold the edges of the
fabric over the cardboard
and glue in place. Do not
worry if it looks a bit
untidy at this stage as the
edges of the fabric will
be covered.

You will need:
colored felt
fabric
fabric glue
cardboard
ribbon
needle and thread

95

3 Cut a piece of
felt 4in x 6in.
Place it on top
of the cardboard. Cut
two lengths of ribbon,
each about 8in long, and
place them in between
the layers, on either side
of the needle case cover.
Stitch the felt to the
folded edge of the fabric,
all round.

4 Cut two pieces of
felt, in contrasting
colors, each
measuring 5in x 3in. Cut
the edges with zigzag scissors, if you have them.
Place on top of each other on the felt side of the
needle case cover and stitch up the center,
through all thicknesses of fabric. The line of
stitching should go up through the gap between
the two pieces of cardboard.

Personalized Gifts

Bath beads or a comb are very acceptable gifts – but you can make them much more special if you add your own personal touch. Here are some ideas.

Comb case

Felt is simple to sew because it doesn't fray. It also comes in a range of bright colors, so you can have fun choosing your own fantastic colorful combination!

You will need:
comb
colored felt
ruler
pen or pencil
needle and thread
zigzag scissors

1 Place the comb on a double layer of felt. Draw a rectangle on the felt, using a ruler to get the edges straight. Cut out, using scissors with zigzag blades.

2 Decorate one of the felt rectangles with felt cutouts, stitched in place.

3 Stitch the two rectangles together around three sides. Cut a notch in the front top edge to make it easier to get the comb out.

Crocodile comb case

Make this in a similar way to the comb case above, but instead of cutting out two rectangles, cut two crocodile shapes from green felt! Decorate with felt shapes and add a googly eye!

Painted jar

Remove the label from a coffee jar and wash the jar thoroughly. Paint a design on the outside of the jar, using special glass paints. You may find it easier if you draw your design on a piece of paper first and place the drawing inside the jar, to act as a guide. Or you may prefer to paint your design freehand. Flowers are an easy motif. Fill the jar with bath beads, bath salts, or, if the lid is watertight, some liquid bubble bath.

Luxury Gifts

Padded coat hangers look pretty and will add a touch of luxury to anyone's wardrobe – while a lavender-filled sachet will make their clothes smell nice!

Padded coat hanger

You will need some ribbon about 2in wide to cover the hangers, and narrower ribbon for decorating. Choose velvet or satin for a really luxurious effect.

You will need:
wooden or plastic coat hanger
scraps of polyester batting
ribbons
pom poms
needle and thread

1 Cut a strip of batting about $^3/4$in longer than the hanger and twice as wide. Fold it over the hanger and stitch the two edges together along the top of the hanger. Stitch the ends together, too.

2 Cut two lengths of wide ribbon, each about $1^1/2$in longer than the hanger. Place one on either side of the hanger and stitch the edges together. At either end, fold the cut edges under and stitch the folds together.

3 Stitch a pom pom to either end of a 10in length of narrow ribbon. Tie the ribbon in a bow around the hook of the hanger.

98

Pot pourri sachet

If you add a loop of ribbon, you can hang this from a coat hanger. Otherwise, it can be placed in a drawer to give clothes a nice perfume and chase away moths!

1 Cut a rectangle of fabric measuring 6¹/2in x 3in. Fold in half and stitch along the bottom and up one side, about ¹/2in from the edges, to form a bag.

You will need:
scrap of cotton fabric
needle and thread
dried lavender
large wooden bead
acrylic paints
paintbrushes
fabric glue
knitting yarn
ribbon
felt

2 Turn right sides out and fill with dried lavender. Fold the raw edge inside along the top, stitch, and gather up the thread.

3 Paint a face on the bead, glue on some yarn for hair, and add a ribbon bow. Stitch the bead to the top of the bag.

99

4 Cut a collar from felt and stitch in place around the neck.

Laundry line card

This card is the perfect accompaniment to the gifts on these pages. Fold a sheet of blue cardboard in half, then cut out shapes from green and brown paper, to make grass and trees. Stick these on place, using a glue stick. Then cut out clothes shapes from paper. Make holes in the card and tie a length of string or cord in place, then attach the clothes to the line, using miniature clothespins, available from stationery stores.

Seasonal Fun

contents

Introduction

Valentine's Day, Easter, a wedding, birthday party, Halloween, or Christmas – all year round there are special times for being creative. Decorating the house for a party? Get out the scissors, glue, and colored paper and start snipping! Want to impress your valentine? Don't just send a card – make them something special! Whatever the occasion, your efforts will be really appreciated by friends and family!

Materials

Paper and paint, cardboard and glue, sticky tape and scissors will all come in useful for seasonal makes! Save all these in a cardboard box so they are handy whenever you feel like being creative.

Save scraps of paper and cardboard– you never know when you might need them. For the projects in *Seasonal Fun*, colored cardboard and paper, tissue and crêpe paper are particularly useful, and self-adhesive film, the transparent kind used for covering books, and the more glittery kind, will also be very useful.

Stock up on colored felt, too. It's available from craft shops and department stores in a wide range of colors. And remember to buy needles, thread, and pins, too, for stitching.

Many special occasions call for a touch of glitter and sparkle, so make sure you have lots of glitter glue to hand. Or maybe just plenty of glue and pots of glitter for sprinkling.

Sequins add a magical sparkle and they come in all sorts of shapes, sizes, and colors. Buying them in small pots can be expensive. You may find it better to buy a big bag of mixed sequins. And fake jewels are useful, too. Choose ones with flat backs that can be glued to greetings cards, fabric, and models.

There are several papier mâché projects in *Seasonal Fun*. This is an easy craft where you use old newspapers and white craft glue diluted with water (one part glue to one part water is about right, or add more or less water to achieve a consistency like cream) to make fantastic models!

Valentine's Day

February 14th is the time to let someone know how much you love them. You may want to send a card – but these love tokens will last much longer!

Felt heart

Send a felt heart to your Valentine this year, instead of a card. Stitch the initial letter of your name on it and see if they can guess who it is from.

You will need:
colored felt
needle and thread
beads
polyester toy batting
scissors
ribbon

1 Cut two heart shapes from bright pink felt and a larger one, with a fancy edging, from pale pink.

2 Decorate one of the heart shapes by stitching on your initial, cut from felt. Add other felt shapes and stitch on beads.

3 Sandwich the pale pink heart shape between the other two pieces and stitch all round, leaving a small gap. Push a little batting inside, to pad out the heart slightly, then finish stitching. Add a loop of ribbon if you like, so the heart can be hung up.

Heart-shaped frame

2 Cover with two layers of papier mâché (see introduction) and when dry, paint it with a layer of watered-down paint so the newspaper shows through slightly.

3 Cut out words or letters from a magazine and paste them in a random pattern all over, then paint a colored border.

105

1 Cut a crown shape from cardboard, then cut a heart-shaped opening in the center.

Heart-throb box

Decorate a heart-shaped card box, from a craft shop, with a photo of your favorite pin-up, adding glitter glue, shiny tape, and a sequin or fake jewel.

Mother's Day

Your mom will really appreciate a home-made present on her special day – as well as a cup of coffee, of course!

Papier mâché tray

Treat your mom to breakfast in bed on a special, home-made tray, painted with her favorite colors.

You will need:
thick cardboard
sticky tape
newspapers
white craft glue
paints

1 Cut a rectangle of cardboard the size you want your finished tray to be. Use a thick cardboard box – stick two layers together if you don't think it will be thick enough. Cut off the corners of the rectangle to give a rounded shape.

2 For the edge of the tray, cut a long strip of card, preferably corrugated cardboard so it will bend easily, and stick it all round the edge of the tray base, using sticky tape.

Warning
Ask an adult to test the strength of your tray before you attempt to use it. It could be dangerous to carry hot food or drink, or breakable china, or glass on it if the tray is not strong enough to hold the weight safely.

3 Dilute white craft glue with water to the consistency of light cream and brush it all over the tray, then stick on torn strips of newspaper. For a really strong result, build up about three or four layers of papier mâché in this way. Leave to dry.

4 Paint the tray in your choice of colors. You could paint a picture of a teapot and teacup, like this one, or perhaps a pattern of flowers?

pier mâché vase

Molding papier mâché around a balloon makes a strong shell – but don't forget it's made of paper, so you must not put water in it!

You will need:
1 long balloon
newspapers
white craft glue
small scraps of cardboard
sticky tape
paints and brushes

1 Blow up the balloon to the size you want your finished vase to be.

2 Dilute the glue with water and brush it all over the balloon. Cover with torn strips of newspaper. You will need to build up at least eight layers of glue and newspaper – preferably ten – to make a really thick papier mâché shell. Leave to dry.

3 Burst the balloon and remove it. Trim both ends of the papier mâché. Decide which will be the base and cut a circle of cardboard to fit, taping it securely in place. On the neck end, roll up a sheet of newspaper into a sausage and tape this in place to form a rim.

4 Apply three more layers of papier mâché to the base and rim. Leave to dry.

5 Paint the vase, first with a base coat of white, then with your choice of pattern. A flower, perhaps? Or a heart to show your mom how much you love her!

Funky flower

As a fun alternative to a fresh flower, this colorful creation can be made in minutes!

You will need:
5 red pipe cleaners
2 yellow pipe cleaners
4 green pipe cleaners

1 Bend each red pipe cleaner into a loop, twisting the ends together, to secure.

2 Place the ends of the red "petals" together in the center and twist one end of a yellow pipe cleaner around all of them, leaving the remainder of the yellow pipe cleaner straight, to form the stem. Wrap the second yellow pipe cleaner round and round to form the flower's center.

3 Loop two green pipe cleaners to form leaves and fold the ends around the stem, then wind the remaining two green pipe cleaners around the stem, securing the leaves in place as you go.

Spring Time

To celebrate the coming of spring, with flowers and new-born lambs – and Easter on the horizon – here are some fun makes, including a container ready to hold some lovely chocolate Easter eggs!

Papier mâché rabbit

Make this bunny to decorate your Easter table, or just as a mascot! The basic shape is molded on two balloons.

1 Blow up two balloons, quite small. Brush each one with diluted craft glue and cover with at least eight layers of newspaper, torn into small strips. Hang up the balloons to dry.

You will need:
2 balloons
newspapers
white craft glue
egg carton
cardboard
paints
paintbrushes

2 Burst the balloons and, trimming off any excess, glue them together to form the rabbit's body and head.

3 Roll up sheets of newspaper into sausages and tape these in place to form the arms, legs, and ears. Stick a cup cut from an egg carton on to the front of the head for the nose. Cover the base with a piece of cardboard cut to size.

4 Cover your model with a further three layers of papier mâché and leave to dry.

5 Paint the rabbit, using acrylic paints or poster paints.

108

Decorated basket

Cut an octagon from cardboard.
Cut eight squares the same measurement
as each side of the octagon and tape in
place using gummed brown parcel tape.
Add a strip of cardboard for a handle.
Paint the basket all over with one color
then paint flowers all round the
edges. Fill with shredded tissue
and tiny chocolate Easter eggs.

Shredded tissue

Roll up a sheet of tissue paper and
flatten it. Cut across into very thin
strips. Gather the strips in your hands
and crumple slightly, then fluff them
out and you have tissue paper straw!

Easter chicks

Cut the body shape from cardboard,
plus a triangle to make the feet.
Glue the two together and cover
with three layers of papier mâché.

When dry, paint the chick
yellow with an orange beak
and feet, adding details with
a black marker pen.

Easter Eggs

Even before the invention of chocolate eggs, decorated eggs were part of the Easter celebrations. You can color eggs, ready to eat, or make more lasting decorations from hollow egg shells.

Painted egg cups

Easter weekend is one of the first big vacations of the year. Dress up the breakfast table with home-made egg cups and felt covers to keep your boiled eggs nice and warm! You can buy wooden egg cups from craft stores – or look in junk stores or charity stores and you may pick one up at a real bargain price!

1 If the wood has been varnished, rub it with sandpaper before you paint it.

2 Use a bright color all over, then add spots and stripes in contrasting colors.

Painted eggs

Empty egg shells make a long-lasting Easter decoration that you can put away and take out year after year.

1 Make a hole at each end of a fresh egg, using a drawing pin, then put your mouth over one of the holes and blow out the contents into a bowl.

2 Wash the egg, inside and out, dry it, then paint with acrylic paints.

Cress eggheads

Save egg shell halves instead of throwing them in the trash can! Wash, draw a face on the shell with felt tip pens, then fill with compost or absorbent cotton. Dampen with water and sprinkle on cress seeds. Do not allow the seeds to dry out, sprinkling them with a few drops of water when necessary, and you will have a crop of cress for your sandwiches in a matter of a few days!

Felt egg cozies

Why not stick with tradition and have boiled eggs for breakfast, keeping them warm with colorful felt egg cozies.

You will need:
colored felt
needle and thread
scissors
pins

1 Cut two basic cover shapes from felt – a sort of semicircular shape. Cut further shapes from felt scraps, to decorate. Choose from flowers, chicks, a bright red heart – whatever you like!

2 Stitch the shapes to one side of the cover. Stitch the two covers together, sandwiching an arch shape with a zigzag edge, cut from a contrasting colored felt.

Party Planning

No matter what time of year, you'll find reason for a celebration! Whether it's your birthday, an anniversary or the first day of the school vacations. here are lots of ideas for festive fun

Paper hats

Here is a really simple way to make a party hat. Why not make one to match the cake frill on the following page?

You will need:
crêpe paper
plain colored paper
patterned wrapping paper
curling gift ribbon
glue stick or double-sided
sticky tape

1 Cut a rectangle of crêpe paper 9½in wide and long enough to go round your head with an extra 1in overlap.

2 Cut a strip of colored paper the same length as the crêpe paper and about 3 inches wide, and a strip of patterned paper 2 inches wide. Use scissors with wiggly or zigzag blades, if you have them. Stick the strips to one long edge of the crêpe paper.

3 Fold over 1 inch on the opposite long edge and stick it down, using a glue stick or double-sided tape. Thread a long length of ribbon through the channel you have created.

4 Now stick the two short sides of the paper together, to form a cylinder. Avoid sticking the very top corners, where the ribbon ends come out.

5 Pull up the ribbon ends tightly, to gather the top of the hat. Tie in a knot, then curl the ends.

Colorful confetti

If you are going to a wedding, why not make your own colorful confetti to throw at the bride and groom? But remember to check with an adult that you will be allowed to throw it at the wedding.

This confetti also looks great scattered over a party table. Simply punch out paper shapes, using a normal hole punch or one with a shaped cutter. Or use scissors with wiggly blades to cut strips.

Crafty tip
Save the pieces of paper you have cut your shapes from, to make party invitations!

113

Flags and Frills

When you're having a party, decorate the house to put everyone in celebratory mood! All you need is colored paper, scissors, string, and glue!

Mexican fiesta flags

At fiesta time, the streets of Mexico are hung with strings of brightly colored tissue paper flags. Make your own to hang in the house or backyard.

You will need:
tissue paper
scissors
string
sticky tape or glue stick

1 Cut tissue paper into rectangles, approximately 8in x 6in.

2 Fold each one in half, then in half again and make lots of little cuts, then open out the paper. Make lots of flags, in a different colors. If you have scissors with zigzag blades, use these to trim the edges, or use a paper punch to make circular holes.

3 Fold the top edge of the flag over a length of string, and glue or tape in place.

Party bunting

Cut triangle shapes from pieces of colored paper and fold the top edge over a length of string.

Paper cake frill

Measure the circumference of your cake and add 1in for overlap. Cut two or three strips of colored tissue paper this length and about 3½in wide. Cut a strip of patterned paper this length and about 2in wide. Stick the paper strips together along the center, using a glue stick. Then use scissors to snip a frill along both edges of the tissue. Wrap the cake frill around your cake and glue the ends together.

Party Fun

Treat your party guests to some fun and games and give them a little souvenir to take home with them...

Balloon heads

Decorated balloons are fun to make and help to create a great party atmosphere. Cut shapes from self-adhesive film or glue on colored paper cutouts using a glue stick or double-sided tape. Make funny faces, or stick on stars, hearts – anything you like! Stand on a cylinder made from cardboard.

Party bags

Transform ordinary brown paper takeaway bags into glamorous party bags using paper cutouts glued in place. Choose simple stars or balloons with real strings and add people's names or initials so you know which bag belongs to whom!

Pin the tail on the elephant

This is a variation on an old party favorite. You could make a picture of any animal you like, perhaps relating it to the theme of your party! Stick the picture to the refrigerator door and the magnetic tail will attach itself like magic! Alternatively, stick the picture to a bulletin board and attach the tail using a thumbtack.

You will need:
large sheets of colored paper in blue and gray
scraps of dark gray and white paper
glue stick
scrap of cardboard
magnet

1 Cut the basic elephant shape from gray paper and stick on to the background. Cut out a separate tail.

2 Cut details from paper scraps and stick them in place. Stick the tail on to a scrap of cardboard and stick a magnet on the back.

3 To play the game, take it in turns to blindfold each other, then try to guess where to place the tail.

Trick or Treat

It has become part of the Halloween tradition to dress up and visit neighbors' houses where, if you are lucky, you may get a treat. Here are some quick dressing-up ideas and a bucket to make, in which to collect your booty!

Collection bucket

Cover a giant waxed paper cup – the kind you get from the cinema, with popcorn or soft drinks – with papier mâché to strengthen it and give a good surface for painting.

You will need:
large paper cup
newspaper
white craft glue
paints
paintbrushes
glitter or glitter glue

1 Brush the cup, inside and out, with diluted craft glue and cover with two or three layers of papier mâché. Leave to dry.

2 Paint the outside black and the inside in a contrasting color.

3 When the paint is dry, decorate with a spider's web, using a glitter glue stick or craft glue painted on and sprinkled with glitter.

Invitations

Cut a pumpkin head shape from orange paper, stick to yellow paper, and cut out again, leaving a small margin of yellow all round the orange shape. Make lots of these and stick to rectangles of thin cardboard, to make Halloween invitations, adding stick-on letters to spell out the word "party."

PARTY

ABCDE
FGHIJK
LMNOP
QRSTU
VWXYZ

Olivia

You can also make place cards for the table by sticking the paper cutouts onto pieces of folded cardboard.

Halloween cards

Send a friend a spooky greeting with a paper cutout card. For a really simple design, cut a skull and crossbones from white paper and stick on to a folded sheet of thin black cardboard. For something a bit more intricate, cut the outline of a spooky landscape, complete with haunted castle, from black paper and stick on to folded orange cardboard. Cut a white paper moon and little ghosts, and black bats.

Devilish horns

Tape horn shapes, cut from cardboard, on to a plastic hair band. Cover this with three layers of papier mâché, to make it sturdy and to give a good surface for painting. When dry, paint the band black and the horns red and you are all set to be a little devil!

spooky Decorations

If you're thinking of having a Halloween party, you may want to decorate your house to create just the right spooky atmosphere.

Pumpkin

Make a pumpkin head in the same way as the cauldron on the opposite page, but without the legs. Instead of a cheese box, the lid of a jelly jar will help to create a flat base so the finished head will stand still without wobbling. Use the same kind of paint technique, dabbing on different shades of orange and red paint, for a mottled effect, then paint a gruesome face before adding a string handle. Use the head as a table centerpiece, with a battery-operated torch inside, or carry it with your when you go trick-or-treating, to fill with treats!

Spooky hangers

Cut ghost and pumpkin head shapes from sheets of craft foam. You should be able to get three ghosts or four pumpkins from a small sheet of foam. Glue on googly eyes and features cut from thin black cardboard, using a glue stick. Then add a pipe cleaner, twirling it around a pencil, to make a spiral hook for hanging up your spooky shapes. Suspend them from a length of string, from door handles – anywhere you like!

Witch's cauldron

A sturdy papier mâché shell is the basis for this cauldron – and with some clever paint effects you can make it look like metal! Stick it in the middle of the table at Halloween and fill it with all kinds of goodies!

You will need:
round balloon
newspapers
cardboard, or cardboard
tubes from kitchen towels
round cheese box
white craft glue
paints, including metallic paints
paintbrushes
wire or string, for handle

1 Blow up the balloon to the size you want your finished cauldron to be.

2 Dilute craft glue with water to the consistency of light cream and brush it all over the balloon. Cover with torn newspaper strips. Build up at least eight layers of papier mâché in this way. For a really strong result, aim for ten layers.

3 When dry, burst the balloon, leaving a thick papier mâché shell. Trim the edge, so you have a bowl shape. Turn the bowl upside down and glue on the lid of the cheese box, to make a base.

4 To make the legs, roll up scraps of cardboard or slit cardboard tubes lengthways and roll up tightly. Cut legs to the required length and stick them in place, using craft glue.

5 When the glue is dry, cover the base and legs with three more layers of papier mâché. Leave to dry.

6 Paint the cauldron, inside and out, with black paint. When dry, add another coat of black if necessary. Then, using a scrap of paper or cloth, rub the surface with a small amount of metallic paint. Metallic gold, bronze, or green are particularly effective and will make the cauldron look as though it's made from old iron!

121

Crafty tips
The papier mâché cauldron or pumpkin head will take several days to make, so start them in plenty of time for Halloween! To protect the finished model, it is a good idea to varnish it. Use diluted white craft glue or a water-based craft varnish.

Countdown to Christmas

Counting the days to Christmas? Here's a special clock to make, to help you keep track of the time, and notepads for jotting down Christmas wish lists.

Advent clock

The clock face has numbers from one to 24, so you can count down to Christmas Day, and award yourself – or someone else – a little present each time you move the pointer!

1 Cut a hexagon shape from cardboard and six squares, the same measurements as each side of the hexagon. Tape one square to each side of the hexagon, then tape edges of squares together, so you have a box. Stand this box on one of its sides and cut pieces of cardboard to construct boxes on either side, using the clock in the picture as a guide.

You will need:
thick cardboard
white craft glue
newspapers
paints
paintbrushes
paper fastener
felt tip pen

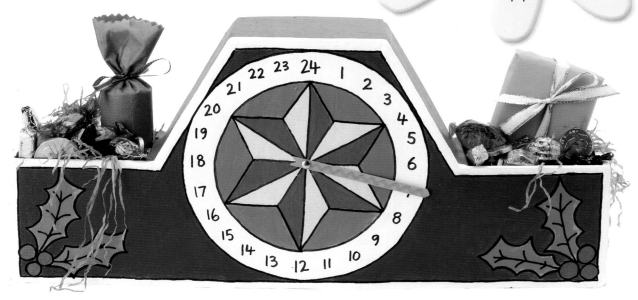

2 Brush the construction with diluted craft glue and cover with torn newspaper strips, building up two or three layers and paying particular attention to edges and joins. Leave to dry.

3 Paint the clock face with a star and the side boxes with Christmas motifs, such as holly.

4 Cut a strip of cardboard and make a hole in one end. Make a hole in the center of the clock face. Use a paper fastener to attach the cardboard strip to the clock face. Write the numbers on the clock face using a felt tip pen.

Christmas notepads

Cut a snowman shape from cardboard. Make the body large enough to stick on a pad of sticky notes and you have somewhere to write all your Christmas lists! Why not make several notepads – a Christmas tree, perhaps, an angel, or a carol singer – and give them away as Christmas presents!

Cards and Wrap

H ome-made cards are much more special than ones from a store, and cheaper too. And while you are at it, why not make your own wrapping paper and gift tags?

Sparkly tree cards

You can create a three-dimensional effect by cutting the tree shapes from thick cardboard.

124

1 Cut triangle shapes for trees. Cover each one by sticking on felt, or pipe cleaners cut into strips, or colored paper.

2 Fold sheets of cardboard in half and decorate the front of each with a rectangle of colored or metallic paper. Stick tree shapes in place.

You will need:
small sheets of colored cardboard
scrap cardboard
scraps of colored, corrugated, and metallic paper
glitter glue, sequins, felt, pipe cleaners, and other trimmings
glue stick

3 Cut bucket shapes from corrugated paper and stick in place.

4 Now you can have great fun decorating the trees, using glitter glue, beads, and sequins.

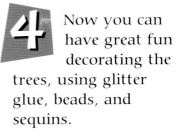

Christmas star cards

Fold colored cardboard in half. Square cards work best with star shapes. Cut stars from colored or textured paper, and decorate with glitter glue and sequins.

Printed giftwrap

Rubber stamps are easy to use and there is a very wide choice available. Or you could cut a shape from a potato and use that instead. Buy plain colored wrapping paper, or brown parcel paper, lay it flat on a table, and print your design all over.

While you have the rubber stamps out, use them to make cards and gift tags. Tear paper into squares and rectangles and print with stamps, then stick onto colored cardboard, adding lengths of string for tying to parcels.

Deck the Halls

On Christmas Eve, make sure you have a stocking ready to hang up! And while you are waiting for Santa to call, keep yourself busy making paper chains to decorate the house!

Christmas stocking

Make your Christmas stocking any size you like and decorate it with your initial so Santa will know whose it is! Fleece fabric is relatively inexpensive and easy to sew because it does not fray. If you don't fancy stitching on the decorations, stick them in place with fabric glue.

You will need:
paper template
pins
scissors
red fleece fabric
colored felt
needle and thread
fabric glue (optional)
sequins
glitter glue
ribbon

1 Cut two stocking shapes from fleece. This is easiest to do if you first make a a paper template and pin it to a double layer of fabric.

2 Choose which side is to be the front, and cut out shapes from felt, to decorate it. Cut out your initial, a wiggly strip to decorate the top, and some squares to represent presents. Stick or stitch all the felt shapes in place.

3 Add a touch of sparkle by stitching or gluing on sequins.

4 With wrong sides together, stitch all round the stocking, leaving the top edge open. The seam will be on the outside of the finished stocking. Add a loop of ribbon, for hanging, if you wish.

Paper chains

This traditional decoration remains popular because it is so easy to make. You can buy colored paper strips in stores but why not cut your own, then you can make your chains any size you like.

Mini Christmas stockings

Little stockings, made from felt, are just the thing for hanging on the tree, or giving to someone, with a little gift inside.

You will need:
colored paper
scissors
glue stick

1 Cut paper into equal sized strips. For a large chain, $8\frac{1}{2}$in x $\frac{3}{4}$in is about right, or for a small chain, $4\frac{1}{2}$ in x $\frac{1}{2}$ in. These measurements allow for $\frac{1}{2}$in overlap.

2 Apply glue to one end of a strip and attach to the other end, creating a ring. For the next and each subsequent strip, first push the strip through the previous loop you have made, before sticking the ends together. In this way, each strip becomes linked to the next, creating a chain.

3 Make the chain as long as you like, and suspend it across a ceiling or drape it over the branches of your Christmas tree.

Festive Table

Christmas dinner is one of the highlights of the year. Dress up your festive table with some fun makes that are sure to make everyone smile!

Snowman

This soft snowman is ideal for decorating the mantelpiece or Christmas table – and he's made from an odd sock!

You will need:
white sock
lid from jar
scraps of yarn
knitting needle
scraps of orange and
black felt
black beads and buttons
needle and thread
polyester toy batting
scissors

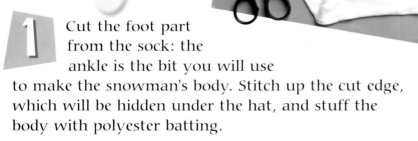

1 Cut the foot part from the sock: the ankle is the bit you will use to make the snowman's body. Stitch up the cut edge, which will be hidden under the hat, and stuff the body with polyester batting.

2 Cut a circle from the remaining part of the sock, slightly bigger than the jar lid. Use this to cover the lid, sticking or stitching the edges of the fabric inside the lid.

3 Tuck the ribbing at the base of the snowman's body inside, then stitch this folded edge to the fabric covering the lid, to form the base.

4 Tie a piece of yarn or thread about a third of the way down the body, to form the head. Stitch black beads in place for a mouth and two beads – or tiny buttons, if you have some – for eyes.

5 Cut a semicircle of orange felt, roll it up, and stitch in place to make a carrot nose.

Festive table mats

Cut out rectangles of wrapping paper measuring 12in x 8in and cover on both sides with transparent self-adhesive film, for wipe-clean table mats.

6 ...ck
...d
...e
...the
smaller circle ...cut
...e

7 Knit a ... on just four stitches and knit a strip long enough to tie around the snowman's neck. If you can't knit, make a felt scarf.

Christmas crackers

Crêpe paper, the perfect choice for making your own crackers, is available in lots of colors, including metallics. Cut rectangles of crêpe paper measuring 12in x 8in. Make sure the creases run along the length of the paper. Place the paper face down and line up three cardboard tubes from toilet rolls along the paper, with a gap of about $\frac{1}{2}$in between each one. Roll the paper around the tubes, gluing the long edge, to form a cylinder. Now tie a piece of string around the paper, in the gap between the tubes. Remove the string and the paper should keep its shape. Decorate each cracker with paper scraps.

Tree Trinkets

A long with the store-bought baubles and tinsel, here are some ideas for home-made trinkets that are sure to make your Christmas tree twinkle!

Shimmering discs

These look equally effective hung from the tree or against a window where they can catch the light. You can buy sheets of acetate from an art supplier – but it's cheaper to save it from packaging such as cookie boxes.

You will need:
pieces of acetate
transparent self-adhesive film
sequins
glitter glue
felt tip pen
hole punch
thread
scissors

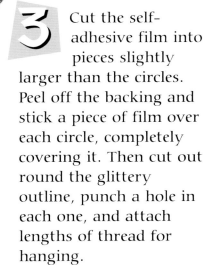

1 Draw circles on the acetate by tracing round a circular object using a felt tip pen.

2 Go over the circles with a line of glitter glue. Then make a pattern of sequins inside each circle, sticking them in place with dots of glitter glue. Leave to dry.

3 Cut the self-adhesive film into pieces slightly larger than the circles. Peel off the backing and stick a piece of film over each circle, completely covering it. Then cut out round the glittery outline, punch a hole in each one, and attach lengths of thread for hanging.

Star topper

With this sparkly star, there is no problem fixing it in place – the tube will slip easily onto the top of the tree! Cut a star shape from thick cardboard. Make slits on either side of a cardboard tube from a toilet roll and insert the star. Brush all over with glue and sprinkle on plenty of glitter. Use different colors for the tube and the star. For a multicolored effect, mix several shades of glitter before shaking on to the star. Leave to dry.

Starry tree decorations

For starry tree decorations, glue scraps of colored foil candy wrappers over both sides of cardboard star shapes. Make a hole in one point, and open out a paperclip to form a hook from which to hang it.

Jazz Up Your Room

Contents

133

Introduction

When it comes to decorating your bedroom, you may or may not have a choice in the color of the walls and carpet, or in the furniture, but there are things you can do to personalize your space.

Interior designers are not just concerned with big things like walls and floors – when designing a room, they know it's the details that make the difference!

In *Jazz Up Your Room*, some of the ideas and quick and easy to achieve, for an almost instant transformation, while others will take a bit more time but will be worth it in the end.

Are you bored with your color scheme, want to add a few splashes of color or touches of glitter and magic? Or are you simply stuck for space, with nowhere to put all your bits and pieces?

Crafty tips

When buying fabric dye, ask a shop assistant for advice. You will need cold water dyes that are suitable for cotton fabrics and are permanent (so they won't wash out). You will probably need to use a special dye fixative and some salt, too. Be sure to check the instructions on the pack of dye before you start.

Do you need some ideas? What about a money box for your loose change; somewhere to store your magazines; containers for pencils, CDs, tissues, and other clutter; and a way of displaying photographs? Or a mobile, or perhaps you would rather make a cozy bed cover and some soft pillows to add a bit of comfort?

WARNING: It's your space, but...

It is wonderful to have the chance to express yourself creatively – but don't get carried away!

You will need to ask someone's permission before you start making any changes. And even if you have been given the go-ahead, always ask the advice of a grown-up before decorating walls, windows, floors, and doors because if you use the wrong paint or glue, for example, you could do irreparable damage!

Fortunately, the ideas in *Jazz Up Your Room* are all pretty safe and do not involve a total room makeover! The ideas in these pages are just accessories to add personalized finishing touches!

Still, grown-up help could be useful with some of the trickier techniques, such as knitting, stitching, printing, and dyeing!

134

Materials

For all the painted projects pictured in these pages, acrylic paints have been used. Acrylics come in a wide range of colors. Some have a matt finish, while some dry to a sheen, and you can even buy a range of metallic colors, including gold, bronze, and silver, which will give a papier mâché vase or picture frame a really smart finish.

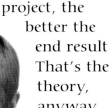

Fabric paints are also useful for quick transformations. These come in pots and can be painted on to fabric with a brush, or printed, using stamps. You may also like to try dyeing fabrics such as sheets, pillowcases, and drapes. Ask your local craft store for advice in buying the right type of dye. Tubes of glossy, pearly, glittery, and metallic fabric paints are also useful, not only for fabric but for squiggling over frames and papier mâché models, and for sticking on fake jewels for a really glitzy effect.

Getting started

If you are making something from papier mâché, bear in mind that it takes time, not only to make the item, but to allow for glue and paint to dry. The projects described here use white craft glue, diluted with water, and strips of newspaper, built up on a base. If the base is constructed from cardboard, you will need to build up about three (or preferably four) layers of glue and paper. If the base is a balloon or mold which will be removed when the papier mâché is dry, aim for seven or eight (or even ten) layers, for a really sturdy and long-lasting result. And the bigger your model, the more craft glue and newspaper you will need – so be prepared!

Sewing and knitting, too, even if they are quite straightforward, may take more time and effort than you think – but the more effort you put into a project, the better the end result! That's the theory, anyway.

135

Making an Entrance

Make a sign for your bedroom door and a bunch of paper flowers to add a splash of color!

Paper flowers

Because crêpe paper can be stretched, it is ideal for making paper flowers as the petals can be pulled into shape. Display the finished blooms in a vase, or fix them around the edge of a mirror. The instructions given will make ten flowers.

You will need:
crêpe paper, 20in wide, in green, pink, yellow, and orange
lengths of wire
sticky tape or double-sided tape

1 Cut lengths of pink, orange, and yellow crêpe paper measuring 24in. Cut each strip lengthways into 5 strips, so each measures 24in x 4in.

2 Fold the pink and orange strips in half, four times, then cut the top third of each folded piece into a v-shape, using plain or zigzag scissors. Cut slits between the petals, cutting down a further third of the width of the strip. Open out.

3 Cut each yellow strip in half, so each measures 12in x 4in. Snip each strip into a fringe, stretch slightly, and roll up around one end of a piece of wire. Fasten in place with sticky tape. This makes the flower center.

4 Now roll a prepared pink or orange paper strip around the flower center, pleating the uncut edge as you go. Tape in place.

5 Cut the green paper into twenty 1in wide strips. Using two strips for each flower, wind the paper around the base of the flower and round the wire stem, stretching it slightly as you go.

6 To finish each flower, stretch the paper petals slightly, pulling them into shape with your fingertips – but take care not to tear the paper!

Grrrr!

To make the shape, draw a circle with a smaller circle inside, then a long, narrow rectangle joined on. Cut out the shape from colored thin cardboard, cutting a gap in the ring so it can be slipped over your door handle. Stick two different colored shapes back to back for a reversible hanger, and put a different message on each side. You could write "do not disturb" or, better still, stick on a scary photo of yourself to frighten everyone away. Or write a welcoming greeting, or stick on a smiley face if you want to encourage visitors!

Warning bells

Star signs

Cut out a five-pointed star from cardboard, then cut out a picture of yourself and stick it in the center. Punch a hole in the top point of the star and tie on a length of ribbon, to hang it up.

Thread small bells on to a length of wire and twist the ends to form a circle. Tie on larger bells using lengths of ribbon and tie on a ribbon loop for hanging. Hang it on your bedroom door and the bells will jingle and tinkle every time someone opens the door!

Storage Solutions

K eep your room tidy with these storage ideas – very easy to make and you could decorate them to co-ordinate with your room scheme!

You will need:
thick card, from a cardboard box
ruler
pencil
sticky tape
gummed brown parcel tape
paint
paintbrush

CD box

This box will hold ten standard compact discs and you can decorate it in any way you like. It is made from cardboard and is easily assembled using gummed brown parcel tape, available from stationers and art stores.

1 Measure and cut pieces of thick cardboard. You will need a piece $5^1/2$in x 5in for the base, 5in x $2^3/4$in for the front, and $6^1/2$in x 5in for the back. For the sides, cut two rectangles, $6^1/2$in x $5^1/2$in then cut these to shape by marking a point 3in along one long side and drawing a curved line from this point to the opposite top corner.

2 Assemble the box, using the finished box, pictured here, as a guide, and sticking pieces together with sticky tape.

3 Cover the whole box, paying particular attention to the corners and edges, with brown parcel tape, moistened with water. Leave to dry for about 1 hour.

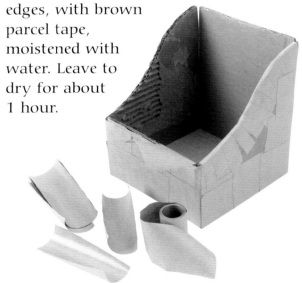

4 Now decorate your box. Paint it in your choice of colors, then paint designs, or stick on paper cutouts, using diluted white craft glue.

Trash can

You don't have to throw your rubbish in this trash can – why not keep treasures in it instead?

You will need:
corrugated cardboard
sticky tape
white craft glue
paintbrush
newspapers
acrylic paints

1 Cut a rectangle of corrugated cardboard measuring 28in x 10in and roll it into a cylinder. Tape the two short sides together.

2 Stand the cylinder on a piece of cardboard and draw round it, to make a circular base. Cut out the base and tape it in place.

139

3 To make the lid, cut a strip of corrugated cardboard about 1^1/4in wide and long enough to go around the bin with a small overlap – about 30in in total. Cut a circle for the top of the lid and tape it to the rim. Cut a strip of cardboard to make a handle, bend it, and tape it in place.

4 Pour some white craft glue into a plastic pot or jelly jar and mix it with an equal amount of water. Brush the mixture all over the trash can and lid, inside and out, then apply pieces of newspaper, torn into strips. Build up about four layers of paper and glue in this way, and leave to dry.

5 Paint the finished trash can with a layer of white paint, leave this to dry, then paint it light gray all over. Mix up several darker shades of gray to paint in the details.

Home Sweet Home

A dd a few homely touches to your room with these fun objects. They are enjoyable to make and each one has a practical use!

House tissue box

Disguise a square box of tissues as a little house and pull tissues out of the "smoking" chimney! Simply measure your box of tissues and cut walls and roof pieces from thick cardboard, slightly larger than the box, so it will fit inside. Assemble the house by sticking the walls and roof together with sticky tape. Don't forget to cut a hole in the roof and make a chimney, too. Then cover your model with four layers of papier mâché. Pour some white craft glue into a plastic pot or jelly jar and mix it with an equal amount of water. Brush the mixture all over, then apply pieces of newspaper, torn into strips. Build up about four layers of paper and glue in this way, and leave to dry. Paint the house using acrylic paints.

House money box

Make this in exactly the same way as the tissue box but add a flat base and cut a slot in the roof. Keep putting money in the slot and your savings will be as safe as houses! When the house is full of money, you can get it out by cutting a hole in the base.

Chair money box

Easily assembled from offcuts of cardboard, you can paint this chair to match your room and even make some little pillows for it, from scraps of fabric.

You will need:
thick cardboard
scissors
corrugated cardboard
sticky tape
paintbrush
white craft glue
sticky tape
newspapers
acrylic paints

1 Cut an 7in square of cardboard, for the base. Cut a rectangle measuring 7in x 5in for the seat and three rectangles 7in x 3^1/2in for the front and sides. Tape all these in place.

2 For the back, cut a rectangle 8in x 7in and tape this in place. Cut another rectangle 7in x 4^1/2in and tape this to the back of the seat. These pieces form the chair back; round off the two top corners of each piece.

3 Cut a strip of corrugated cardboard 2^1/2in wide and long enough to go over the top of the chair back – about 18in – and tape this in place. Cut a slot in the center.

4 For the chair arms, cut two 5in squares of corrugated card, roll them up, and tape in position.

5 Brush the whole structure with diluted craft glue and apply torn newspaper. Build up at least four layers. Leave to dry.

5 Paint the chair white, to cover up the newsprint, then paint it in your choice of color. To paint daisies, first print the flowers centers by dipping the flat end of a pencil in yellow paint and stamping spots all over the chair. Add white petals by dipping a soft paintbrush in paint and laying the brush fairly flat, to make a petal-shaped impression.

141

On the Shelf

A clock and bookends will add a touch of class to your room. The clock really works and the bookends can be made to represent any letters of the alphabet!

Cardboard clock

This elegant clock is simply constructed out of cardboard. Buy the battery-operated clock works from a craft supplier.

You will need:
thick cardboard
round cardboard or plastic lid
scissors
plastic bag
sand or pebbles
corrugated cardboard
white craft glue
sticky tape
2 paper pulp balls
newspapers
acrylic paints
paintbrush
sponge
battery-operated
clock works

142

1 For the base, construct a box from cardboard, with the top and base measuring 8in x $3^{1}/_2$in, and the sides 2in high. Fill a plastic bag with sand or pebbles, seal it, and place inside the box, to give the finished clock some weight and to prevent it from toppling over.

2 For the front of the clock, cut a rectangle of cardboard 14in x $8^{1}/_2$in. Place the battery pack for the clock works in the center of the card, draw around it, and cut this shape out. Draw a line across, $3^{1}/_2$in down from the top edge of the cardboard, then draw a circle in the center with a radius of about $2^{1}/_2$in, using the clock on this page as a guide. Cut out the shape at the top. Draw around this shape on to a piece of cardboard 8in x $3^{1}/_2$in; this piece will go at the back. For the sides, cut strips of cardboard 10in x $1^{1}/_2$in. Tape these side pieces to the weighted box, then tape the front of the clock in place and the back piece.

3 Cut a strip of corrugated cardboard 1$\frac{1}{2}$in wide and long enough to go across the top of the clock, fitting around the curved shape – about 10$\frac{1}{2}$in. Then tape on two small triangles at the top back corners, to help make the structure really strong.

4 For the columns at the sides, cut two 11in squares of corrugated cardboard and roll them up tightly. Tape in place and top with paper pulp balls. For the clock face, use a round cardboard or plastic lid glued in place. Make a hole in the center, through both lid and cardboard, so you can insert the clock works later.

5 Dilute white craft glue with an equal amount of water and brush the mixture all over the clock, then apply pieces of newspaper, torn into strips. Build up about four layers of paper and glue in this way, and leave to dry.

6 Paint the finished clock white, then dab on pale blue paint with a sponge. Cut out numbers and stick them on, or paint them directly on to the clock face.

143

7 Fit the clock works, which should fit snugly into the hole you have cut.

Alphabet bookends

Cut your chosen letter from thick cardboard. Make it about 8in high. You will need two or three shapes exactly the same. Glue them together to make a thick letter shape.

Then cut the base, 6$\frac{1}{2}$in x 4in and back piece, 7$\frac{1}{2}$in x 4in. Join these together, then tape the letter in place. Cover the structure with four layers of papier mâché (see step 5 of the clock), leave to dry, then paint in your choice of bright colors.

Pillows

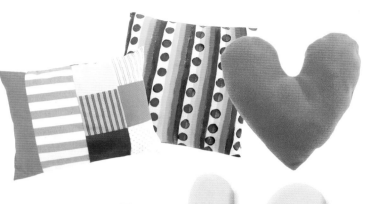

These pillows will add color and comfort to your room and are a great way to express your creativity!

Painted pillow

Recycle an old sheet or pillowcase to make this colorful cushion. If you are using new fabric, wash and dry it before you start painting.

1 Lay the white fabric flat, on plenty of newspaper. Paint dark red stripes, $2^1/2$in apart. Then paint orange stripes. By the time you have done these, the dark red ones should be dry and you can paint bright red stripes, then yellow ones.

2 Pour a little blue paint on to a saucer or plastic lid, dip a cork into the paint, and use it to print large dots in the spaces between the stripes you have painted.

3 Leave to dry completely, then press with a hot iron (you may need an adult's help with this), according to the instructions on the pots of fabric paint. This will fix the color into the fabric and make it permanent.

You will need:
white cotton fabric, 16in square
newspaper
fabric paints
paintbrush
cork
needle and thread
red cotton fabric, 15in square
14in square cushion pad

4 Trim the edges of the painted fabric so you are left with a square measuring 15in. Place it on top of the red fabric square, painted side facing inward, and stitch round three sides, $1/2$in from the edges. Turn right sides out, insert the cushion pad, tuck in the raw edges, and sew the opening closed.

Crafty tips
Make your own cushion pad from scrap fabric, filling it with polyester batting. The advantage of using a cushion pad is that you can remove your cover when it is dirty, and wash it.

144

Patchwork cushion cover

You don't have to be an expert at sewing to stitch this – it's really easy! You just have to be able to stitch two pieces of fabric together in a straight line, by hand or using a sewing machine if you have access to one.

You will need:
scraps of cotton fabrics
needle and thread
16in x 12in cushion pad

Heart cushion

Use soft, fluffy fleece to make this cover. Cut a heart shaped template from paper and use this as a pattern to cut out two heart shaped pieces of fleece. Stitch them together, $1/2$in from the edges, leaving a small opening. Turn right sides out, stuff with polyester batting and sew the opening closed.

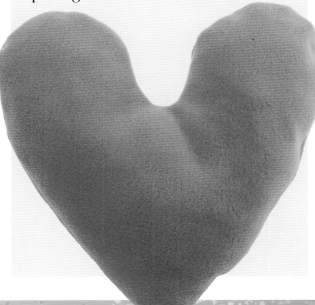

1 Cut six 4in squares of fabric, all different. Try to combine your own selection of plain, striped, and printed designs. Stitch three squares together to form a strip, with $1/2$in seams, stitch another strip of three squares then stitch the two strips together.

2 Now cut a rectangle of fabric 13in x $5^1/2$in and stitch it to one side of the piece you have made. Cut another piece, 13in x $3^1/2$in and join this on, too. You should now have a piece measuring 16in x 13in. Cut a plain piece of fabric this size, for the back of the cover, place it on top of the patchwork, right side facing inward, and stitch round three sides, $1/2$in from the edges.

3 Turn right sides out, insert the cushion pad, tuck in the raw edges, and sew the opening closed.

Fabric Fun

Decorate drapes or bed linen with colorful printed designs. Be as bold as you like with color, using store-bought stamps or home-made ones.

Printed border

Use plain colored cotton fabrics and fabric paints to create a colorful border. New fabric should be washed and dried before printing.

1 Lay the fabric flat on plenty of newspaper.

2 Cover the surface of your chosen stamp with fabric paint, using a brush or roller. Test the stamp on a spare scrap of fabric first, then print the shape, repeating it at intervals.

You will need:
plain colored cotton fabrics
newspaper
fabric paints
paintbrush or roller
rubber stamps
cork

3 Stamp a second design, if you like, using a different color. You can stamp spots using a cork dipped in paint.

4 Leave to dry completely, then press with a hot iron (you may need an adult's help), according to the instructions on the pots of fabric paint. This will fix the color into the fabric and make it permanent.

Crafty tips
To make your own stamp, cut out a shape from a thin sheet of foam rubber. You can buy craft foam, sometimes known as neoprene, from art and craft stores and it is easy to cut with scissors. Or you could use a new dish-washing sponge. The foam rubber can be thin. Stick your cutout shape to a block of wood, using double-sided foam sticky pads.

146

Drape with printed border

Stitch a printed strip of fabric to a larger piece of plain or patterned cotton fabric, to make a drape. Hem all round and fold over about 1in at the top, to form a channel. Thread a length of plastic-covered curtain wire through this channel and you can hang up your drape across a window or maybe along the edge of a shelf, to hide any clutter! You could also stitch printed borders to sheets or pillowcases.

Potato print vest

While you are in the mood for printing, why not decorate a vest with a fish motif, or make up your own designs.

You will need:
cotton vest
newspaper
potato
knife
fabric paints
paintbrush

147

1 Lay the vest flat on a surface protected with plenty of newspapers. Place a thick wad of newspaper inside the vest so the paint doesn't soak through to the back.

2 Slice the potato in half and cut out a fish shape from one half. You may need the help of an adult to do this.

3 Brush the surface of the potato with fabric paint and press it into position on the T-shirt. Repeat to make lots of printed fish shapes.

4 Cut away parts of the potato, leaving stripes, brush the surface of the potato with fabric paint in a second color, and print stripes on each fish.

5 Cut more shapes from the potato: fins and bubbles, for example, and print these. Leave until the paint is completely dry, then press the vest, using a hot iron and following the instructions on the pot of fabric paint, to fix the color.

Bed Time

Instead of plain pillows, why not have patterned ones? Decorate them yourself, using fabric paint or dye.

Tie-dye pillowcase

Start with a plain, pale colored pillowcase and a tin of cold water dye, suitable for cotton fabrics.

1 Wash the pillowcase, wring out most of the water, but leave it damp.

2 Tie pebbles into the fabric, tying tightly with short lengths of string.

You will need:
cotton pillowcase
cold water dye
small pebbles
string
rubber gloves
plastic bucket

148

3 Make up the dye powder according to the packet instructions and put it in the plastic bucket. Protecting your hands with rubber gloves, immerse the pillowcase in the dye and leave it for the recommended length of time – about 1 hour.

4 Remove the pillowcase from the dye and rinse in cold water until the water runs clear, then remove the string and pebbles. Wash the pillowcase in hot, soapy water, rinse, and dry.

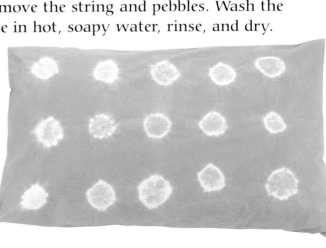

Printed pillowcase

Use fabric paint to decorate a pillowcase. The one in the picture was printed with rubber-stamped stars and a moon shape cut from a potato.

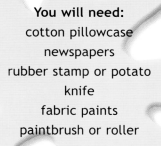

 Lay the pillowcase flat on a surface protected with plenty of newspaper. Place a thick wad of newspaper inside the pillowcase so the paint doesn't soak through to the back.

2 Slice the potato in half and cut out a moon shape from one half. You may need the help of an adult to do this.

3 Brush the surface of the potato with fabric paint and press it into position on the pillowcase. Repeat to make lots of printed moon shapes.

4 Stamp stars using a different color. You can cut your own star shape from the other half of the potato, or use a rubber stamp if you have one.

149

5 Leave to dry completely, then press with a hot iron, (you may need an adult's help) according to the instructions on the pots of fabric paint. This will fix the color into the fabric and make it permanent.

Pyjama bag

Make a simple bag from two pieces of striped fabric, 18in x14in, stitched together round three sides. Cut two pieces of spotty fabric 18in x 5$\frac{1}{2}$in, fold and stitch to the top of the bag and thread with cord, to make drawstrings. Neaten the ends with fabric scraps.

Very Cozy

A cozy patchwork blanket requires the most basic of knitting skills, while a woolly snake draft excluder can be made from old clothes!

Patchwork blanket

Collect balls of double knitting yarn in a variety of colors. You could use all the colors of the rainbow, or stick to shades of your favorite colors – such as purples, pinks, and greens! One 2oz ball of yarn will make three or four squares, depending on how tightly or loosely you knit!

You will need:
number 6 knitting needles
double knitting yarn
tapestry needle

150

Crafty tip
To make 42 squares, you will need approximately twelve 2oz balls!

1 Cast on 25 stitches and knit 45 rows. You should have a square of knitting. If your knitting is not square, you may have to knit a few more rows (or a few less!).

2 Keep knitting until you have a whole pile of squares. Each time you finish a square, break off the yarn leaving a piece about 10in long. These long ends will be threaded into your tapestry needle and used to sew the squares together.

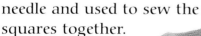

3 The blanket pictured is made from 42 squares. Stitch six squares together in a row. Repeat until you have seven strips, each made of six squares, then join the strips together.

Snake draft excluder

If the wind whistles under your bedroom door or window, this is just what you need. Or you may just want it as a mascot or another cuddly toy! To make a snake, simply cut the foot off a long sock or the sleeve off an old sweater. Make the front end of the snake by stitching $1/2$in from the cut edge and pulling the thread to gather the fabric. Tuck the raw edges inside and stitch a tongue in place, cut from red felt. Stuff the tube with polyester batting, then stitch the edges of the cuff together neatly. Finally, stitch on eyes cut from black and white felt.

Cozy hat

You could use yarn left over from your blanket to make a stylish hat! Using number 6 knitting needles, cast on 160 stitches. Knit about 70 rows in stripes of different colors. Cast off, then fold the knitting in half and stitch the two short sides together. Stitch across the top.

Add a couple of knitted strips and tie them together, then roll up the edge to make a brim.

In the Frame

Instead of sticking pictures straight on your bedroom wall, frame them! They'll look good and you are less likely to damage the wall.

Junk frame

If your room is a mess, you are likely to find all the things you need to decorate this frame scattered all over the floor! Just collect together plastic toys, combs, pencils, anything you don't have a use for, then follow the simple instructions!

You will need:
plain wooden frame
sandpaper
white craft glue
small wooden or
plastic objects
spray paint (optional)

1 Make sure your frame is clean and dust-free. If it is varnished or painted, you may need to rub it all over with sandpaper to give a good surface for gluing and painting.

2 Dab the frame with generous blobs of glue and place the toys and other objects in position. Use plenty of glue. The glue will stay wet for long enough to alter your arrangement if you have to. Then leave it to dry. Although the glue is white when you apply it, it will become clear as it dries.

3 Leave the frame as it is, or paint it. You may need an adult's help or permission before using spray paint. Make sure the room is well ventilated or do it outside. Protect the surrounding area with plenty of newspaper and read the instructions on the can.

Glitter frame

Look in craft stores or junk stores for small wooden frames. If your frame is painted or varnished, rub it all over with sandpaper. Then paint it with white acrylic paint. Leave to dry and brush with white craft glue. Stick fake jewels in place, then sprinkle with a thick layer of glitter while the glue is still wet – use more than one color if you wish.

Jewel frame

Simple but effective, this frame is suitable for a standard size photograph but you could make it bigger or smaller, if you prefer.

You will need:
thick cardboard
scissors
white craft glue
gold acrylic paint
paintbrush
glitter glue (optional)
fake jewels

1 Cut a rectangle of cardboard measuring 12in x 10in, then cut a hole in the center 6in x 4in (or slightly smaller if you prefer).

2 Cut circles of cardboard $1^3/4$in in diameter and glue firmly in place around the edge of the frame using glue. Leave to dry.

3 When the glue is dry, paint the frame all over with gold paint. You may need to apply two coats.

4 Stick a fake jewel on each of the circles, using glue glue or glitter glue. Tape your photograph to the back of the frame.

Going Wild!

Accessories decorated with animal prints can make your room look wildly glamorous – or just wild!

Tiger bowl

Make a papier mâché shell and add a base, then decorate it with tiger stripes or your own favourite animal print.

1 Blow up the balloon to the size you want your finished bowl to be and stand the knotted end in a jelly jar, taping it in place.

You will need:
round balloon
white craft glue
newspapers
cardboard tubes from toilet roll
corrugated cardboard
paintbrush
acrylic paints

2 Dilute white craft glue with water and brush it over three-quarters of the balloon. Cover with torn newspaper strips. Build up at least eight layers of papier mâché in this way. For a really strong result, aim for ten layers. When dry, burst the balloon, leaving a thick papier mâché shell.

3 Trim the edge, so you have a bowl shape. Turn it upside down and glue the cardboard tube in place. Add a strip of corrugated cardboard, rolled around the end of the tube, to make a base.

4 Cover the base and the trimmed edge of the bowl with three more layers of papier mâché. Leave to dry.

5 Paint the bowl, inside and out, with white paint, to cover the newsprint and give a good base for painting. Then paint it two shades of yellowy-orange. Leave to dry and paint on black stripes. Paint the inside in a color of your choice.

Giraffe frame
To make the frame, glue a small square box or box lid inside a slightly larger one and cover the gap between the two with cardboard strips, to create a frame. Paint the edge of the frame with a giraffe pattern. Paint the background and the inside of the frame with a scene including a painted giraffe, then place plastic giraffes in the frame for a 3D effect.

Leopard vase

This is also made from papier mâché but this time the shape is molded around a long balloon!

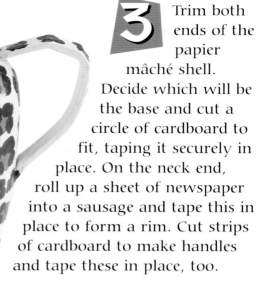

You will need:
1 long balloon
newspapers
white craft glue
corrugated cardboard
sticky tape
paints and brushes

1 Blow up the balloon to the size you want your finished vase to be.

2 Follow step 2 of the method for making the Tiger bowl.

3 Trim both ends of the papier mâché shell. Decide which will be the base and cut a circle of cardboard to fit, taping it securely in place. On the neck end, roll up a sheet of newspaper into a sausage and tape this in place to form a rim. Cut strips of cardboard to make handles and tape these in place, too.

4 Apply three more layers of papier mâché to the base, handles and rim. Leave to dry.

5 Paint the vase, first with a base coat of white, then with two shades of yellowy-orange. Dab with spots of brown, then outline these spots with dabs of black paint, using the vase pictured here as a guide.

155

Magazine boxes

Recycle cereal, washing powder, or cat food boxes by covering them with wrapping paper and you'll have somewhere to store all your magazines, booklets or catalogs! Cut off the top flaps, then cut diagonally across the front and back of the box. Place the box on a sheet of gift wrap and draw each side, adding a margin of about ³/4in. Stick the paper to the box, using a glue stick – or use self-adhesive paper – and tuck the excess paper inside the box. Make a set of boxes in different sizes and line them up on a shelf. You could label each box with its contents.

Hanging Around

The projects on this page should be suspended from the ceiling, window frame, or doorway, or from below a shelf, for maximum impact!

Dream catcher

Hang this above your bed to filter out all the bad dreams and let only the good ones through!

You will need:
wooden ring from embroidery frame
cotton yarn
wooden beads
feathers

1 Start by binding the whole ring with yarn. Cut a long length of yarn, knot one end around the ring, and wind the yarn round and round. You may have to use more than one piece of yarn, knotting the ends to the ring to fasten them off.

2 Now make loops with the yarn, all the way round, knotting the yarn firmly to the ring as you go.

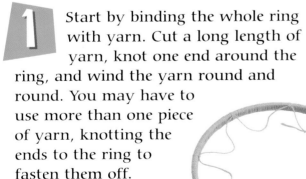

3 Tie a long length of yarn to one of the loops then working clockwise, loop the end of the yarn through the next loop, then over itself, then pull quite tight. Repeat this with the next loop and the next, and so on all round.

4 When you have threaded the yarn through every loop, start on the next row, doing exactly the same, and continuing in a spiral until you are near the center of the ring.

5 Thread a few beads on to the yarn and proceed as before until you reach the center, then knot off the yarn.

6 Do not cut the end of the yarn yet, but thread a few beads on to it and tie a feather to the end. The beads should slip over the feather quite easily.

7 Add further lengths of yarn, knotted to the ring, threaded with beads and with feathers on the end. Then add a loop of yarn to the opposite side of the ring, for hanging.

Bead curtain

Choose a length of wooden doweling the width you want your curtain to be. To it, tie lengths of strong cotton yarn, about 1in apart, and about one and a half times the length you want your finished curtain to be. Thread beads on to each string, making knots in between to create spaces between the beads. Use glass or plastic beads, or even plastic drinking straws cut into short lengths. Hang your finished curtain from two hooks, placed either side of your window or doorway.

157

Sun and moon mobile

Use a round lid from a plastic tub, as a base. Then roll up or crumple small pieces of tissue paper or kitchen paper, dip them in diluted white craft glue, and use them to mold features. On one side, make a sun face, with a circular rim, nose, cheeks, and eyebrows.

On the other side, mold the shape of a new moon, again with nose, mouth, and other features. Leave to dry, then paint with acrylics. Add a length of ribbon for hanging.

Flower Power

If pink is your choice of color for your bedroom you will love these pretty accessories, all easy to make and paint!

Flower bowl

You will need a large bowl on which to mold your papier mâché. A plastic bowl is best but whatever you choose will be protected by layers of plastic and should not come to any harm.

1 Cover the bowl, inside and out, with at least two layers of plastic wrap. This is to protect the surface from the glue and paper.

2 Dilute white craft glue with water and brush it over the plastic wrap on the inside of the bowl. Cover with torn newspaper strips. Build up at least eight layers of papier mâché in this way. For a really strong result, aim for ten layers. When dry, lift out the papier mâché shell and peel off the plastic wrap.

3 Make a second bowl, this time using the outside of your mold. Brush glue over the plastic wrap on the outside of the bowl and build up eight or ten layers of papier mâché, as before.

4 Put the smaller bowl inside the larger one, with a layer of crumpled newspaper in between, to separate the two layers by about 3/4in.

5 Trim the edges of the papier mâché bowls, so they are level, and tape them together across the top. To make a rim, roll up a newspaper into a sausage and tape this in place. Apply three more layers of papier mâché to the rim. Leave to dry.

6 Paint the bowl, inside and out with white paint, to cover the newsprint and to give a good base for painting. Then paint it pink all over. Leave to dry and paint on flowers in the colors of your choice.

Funky flower vase

Blow up a long balloon to the size you want your finished vase to be. Brush all over with diluted white craft glue and cover with torn newspaper strips. Build up at least eight layers. When dry, burst the balloon, leaving a papier mâché shell. Trim both ends with scissors. Tape a circle of cardboard to the base and a roll of paper to the top to form a rim. Make handles from strips of cardboard. Cover with a further three layers of papier mâché. When dry, paint your vase with a base coat of white paint, then with the color of your choice. Finally, add a funky flower motif.

Flower frame

Paint a plain wooden frame pink, then decorate with painted flowers. If the frame is already painted or varnished, rub it all over with sandpaper to give a good surface before you start painting. Start with two coats of pink acrylic, then print spots, using the end of a pencil dipped in paint. Paint a flower picture to match, to place inside your funky frame.

Jean Genius

If you are the kind of person who loves to live in jeans, why not recycle an old pair to make some great accessories for your room?

Denim pot

Cut a piece of denim fabric long enough to go around an empty canister (from custard powder or drinking chocolate), adding $1/2$in for an overlap, and about $1^1/2$in wider than the height of the can. Spread the outside of the can with a very thin layer of fabric glue, leave for 5 minutes, until tacky, then wrap the fabric around the can, having one long edge of the fabric level with the bottom edge of the can. When the glue is dry, pull threads out of the fabric to fringe the top edge, and tie a length of ribbon around the can, to decorate it.

Denim pillow

Cut two 10in squares from an old pair of jeans. Patch any holes. Remove one of the back pockets from the jeans and stitch to one of the squares. Stitch the squares together, right sides inward, around the of the sides. Turn right sides out, stuff with polyester batting, then sew up the gap. Decorate with glittery fabric paint.

Denim bulletin board

If you haven't got a piece of old jeans fabric big enough, buy a denim remnant. Cover up an old board, or buy a cheap one and customize it.

You will need:
bulletin board with frame
sandpaper
acrylic paint
paintbrush
denim fabric
white craft glue
thumb tacks
ribbons

1 Remove the board from its frame. If it has been varnished or painted, rub it all over with sandpaper before painting. Paint it with a bright colored acrylic and leave to dry.

2 Meanwhile, cut a piece of denim large enough to cover one side of the board, with about 3in overlap all round. Spread one side of the board with a thin layer of craft glue. Leave for 10 minutes, until slightly dried and tacky, then cover with the fabric. Leave to dry.

161

3 Turn the frame over and fold the excess fabric to the wrong side of the board, securing it in place by gluing, as before, or pinning, using thumb tacks.

4 Lay lengths of ribbon across the front of the board in a criss-cross pattern. Where pieces cross, secure with a thumb tack. Pin the ends of the ribbons to the back of the frame.

5 Replace the board in its newly painted frame. Tuck pictures behind the ribbons for a colorful display.

Sparkly Splendor

Silver, gold, glitter, sequins, and jewels will add a little bit of opulence to any room!

Jeweled bowls

Fake jewels are available from craft stores. Acrylic paint is available in a range of metallic and pearlized colors.

You will need:
round balloon
white craft glue
paintbrush
newspapers
cardboard rings
(from sticky tape rolls)
metallic acrylic paints
fake jewels

1 Blow up the balloon to the size you want your finished bowl to be. Stand the knotted end of the balloon in a jelly jar, taping it in place.

2 Dilute white craft glue with water and brush it over three-quarters of the balloon. Cover with torn newspaper strips. Build up at least eight layers of papier mâché in this way. For a really strong result, aim for ten layers. When dry, burst the balloon, leaving a thick papier mâché shell.

3 Cut the shell in half, to make two bowls. Trim the edges to create wavy shapes. Turn the bowls upside down and glue a cardboard ring in place, to make a base. Cover the base and the cut edges of the bowls with three more layers of papier mâché. Leave to dry.

4 Paint the bowls, inside and out, with white paint, to cover the newsprint and to give a good base for painting. Then paint them gold or silver.

5 When the paint is dry, glue on fake jewels using blobs of glue.

162

Glitter box

You can buy cardboard boxes in various shapes and sizes, from craft stores, or you may find a round chocolate box with a lid. The box doesn't have to be round – any box with a lid can be painted and decorated in this way and look just as effective.

1 Paint the box all over with one or two coats of acrylic paint.

2 Draw shapes using blobs of glitter glue and stick fake jewels in position.

3 Add more blobs of glitter glue, in one or more colors, and more jewels, or sequins, or both, until you are pleased with the result. Leave to dry overnight.

163

Glitter glue
Glitter glue is available in a range of colors – just squeeze it straight out of the tube to make patterns, dots, and swirls. While it is wet, you can push jewels and sequins in the the glue. You can also sprinkle wet glue with dry glitter in different colors, for a really sparkling, multi-layered effect.

Dressing Up

contents

165

Introduction

Dressing Up is about everyday style as well as fancy dress for those special occasions! Make some jewelry, a hair band, or a bag – or make a whole outfit, it's up to you! And it's such fun to wear something you have made yourself!

Are you going to a party? You may want to make a fantasy costume, something magical or comical? Should it be something quick, easy, and cheap, conjured up from scraps of paper and plastic, or something that requires a bit more time and effort, using fancy fabrics and a little bit of skill with a needle and thread?

Or do you simply want to add to your day-to-day wardrobe? It may be that you want to jazz up an existing outfit, or make some eye-catching accessories. You could start with something easy, like a simple necklace or bracelet, or try something a bit more challenging like a hair slide, hat,

or bag. Whatever you decide to do, you'll find that all the ideas in *Dressing Up* are fun and creative!

Sew simple

Even if your sewing skills are fairly basic, accessories such as hats and bags – or even whole outfits – are not that hard to make. The instructions given in the following pages are easy to follow and an adult should be able to show you the basic stitches needed.

Fabrics and other materials

You don't have to spend a fortune on fabrics. Check out your wardrobe first of all, for clothes you have grown out of. Perhaps you can recycle them? Shirts, sweatshirts, vests, jeans, and even underwear and pantyhose can all be given a new lease of life!

Rummage sales and charity stores are a good source of materials. An old sparkly evening dress, perhaps, that can be cut up and made into a fairy tutu? Or some broken necklaces that can be taken apart, and the beads rethreaded?

Dyes and fabric paints

A plain vest that you are bored with could be given a whole new lease of life with some dye or a painted design. Craft stores are the place to go to find a selection of dyes. Don't be afraid to ask an assistant for advice if you are not sure which kind to buy. And get the help or permission of an adult before embarking on any messy activities like dyeing. Fabric paints are great fun to use. There is the kind sold in pots, for painting or printing, and those sold in tubes, which can be pearly, puffy, or glittery, and are useful for squiggly designs or for sticking sequins and jewels to fabrics and craft projects.

Be prepared

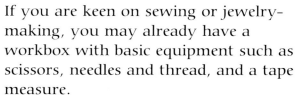

If you are keen on sewing or jewelry-making, you may already have a workbox with basic equipment such as scissors, needles and thread, and a tape measure.

It's useful to have several pairs of scissors, one for cutting fabric and another for cutting paper etc (tie a different colored ribbon around the handle of each pair to remind yourself which is which). Cutting paper can blunt scissor blades and you need sharp scissors to cut through most fabrics. But be sure to be very careful with them – never carry scissors around and always put them away safely out of the reach of younger children.

Keep pins and needles in matchboxes or plastic film canisters. You will need a few small, sharp needles for sewing fabric, a long, fine one with a small eye for threading tiny beads, and a larger, thicker, blunter one for stringing larger beads on thicker thread or yarn.

Visit your local craft store or bead store for beads in all shapes and sizes, strong beading thread, and fastenings for necklaces or brooches. While you

are there, you could also buy colored felt, ribbons, safety pins, feathers, fake jewels, and fabric flowers.

Fabric stores often sell remnants – small pieces of fabric, usually offered at a reduced price – so look out for scraps of interesting fabrics, including net, fleece, and animal prints. And ask any adults you know who do sewing, to save leftover scraps for you.

And for every kind of craft activity – not only the ones on the following pages – it is always useful to have a stock of paper (plain and textured), paints (preferably acrylics), glue (white craft glue, fabric glue, and glue stick), sticky tape, wire, and string.

Playing Pirates

A hoy there! Take an old sweater and pair of pants, plus some pieces of fabric, and create a costume for sailing the high seas!

Pirate flag

This flag, known as the Jolly Roger, struck terror into sailors' hearts. No self-respecting pirate would be without his or her skull and crossbones!

168

You will need:
black cotton fabric
needle and black thread
pencil and paper
white cotton fabric
fabric glue
wooden stick

1 Cut a rectangle of black fabric measuring 16in x 12in. Turn under $1/2$in all round, to form a hem. Stitch.

2 Draw a skull and crossbones on paper. When you are satisfied with your design, cut it out, and pin it to the white fabric. Cut out the shapes and glue them to the black fabric.

3 Fold over $3/4$in on one side of the flag, and stitch, to form a channel. Stitch across the top. Insert the stick.

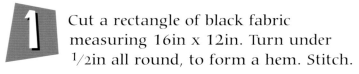

Pirate sweater

Cut the sleeves and neck from a striped sweater or vest. Using the paper template from the flag, cut a skull and crossbones from white fabric and glue to the front of the sweater, using fabric glue.

Eye patch

Make a simple eye patch from black cardboard. Punch holes and thread a length of elastic, a shoe lace, or black tape through for tying.

Pirate scarf

Cut a square of fabric measuring 26in, then fold this in half lengthways, to make a triangle. Wrap the long edge around your head and knot the pointed ends at the back or side. You could also make a sash to go around your waist – cut a strip of fabric measuring 48in x 12in, fold it lengthways, and tie it around your waist.

Pirate pants

Cut off the legs from a pair of jeans, to below knee length. Cut slits up the outside seams. Stitch on colorful squares of fabric, to make knee patches.

Hat Tricks

On a cold day, you'll want to wear a nice, warm hat – particularly one you have made yourself! Try one of these – they are easy to make but sure to impress!

Heart hat

This hat is constructed from two squares of fleece fabric. When buying fleece, ask for a 12in length, which should be enough to make two or three hats. Alternatively, cut up an old sweatshirt or tracksuit pants. Decorate your hat with a heart or your own choice of motif.

You will need:
two 12in squares of purple fleece fabric
small scrap of red fleece
needle and thread

1. Lay the squares together and stitch up two opposite sides, about 1/2in from edges.

2. Turn right sides out, so seams are on the inside, then flatten so that seams are in the center.

3. Cut a heart shape from the red fleece and stitch on top of one of the seams.

4. Fold inside out again, and stitch along the top. Turn right sides out and fold the two top corners to the center, securing them in place with a few firm stitches.

5. Fold over 3/4in along the bottom edge, and stitch. Roll up this edge, to form a brim.

Snuggly scarf

For the simplest scarf, cut a rectangle of fabric measuring 48in x 7in. Snip a fringe at either end, with each strip about 1/2in wide. Knot the end of each strip.

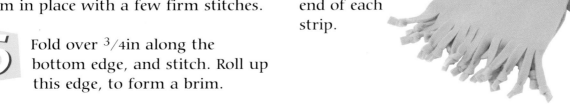

Tassel hat

Make this in exactly the same way as the heart hat but without the motif at the front. Do not stitch the top corners to the center, but cut 14 strips of red fleece, $4\frac{1}{2}$in x $\frac{1}{2}$in. Place six strips together and tie a strip around the center, tightly, to make a tassel. Stitch the tassels to the two corners.

Pixie hat

This pointed hat is made by joining four pieces together. You could cut each section from a different colored fleece!

You will need:
blue fleece fabric, at least 26in x 14in
scrap of green fleece fabric
paper and pencil
pins
needle and thread

171

1 Start by making a paper template. Draw a rectangle 6in x 3in. From the center of one of the long sides, draw a line 9in long. Join the end of this line to the two corners of the rectangle.

2 Pin the template to your fabric and cut out four fabric pieces.

3 Stitch the pieces together, to form a cone. Fold up $\frac{3}{4}$in along the bottom edge and stitch, to form a hem, then roll up to form a brim.

9in

3in   6in

4 Make a tassel from three blue and three green strips, and stitch to the top of the hat.

Fairy Fun

Most girls like to put on a pair of wings and wave a wand. It's easy to create your own little bit of fairy magic with these home-made fairy accessories.

Fairy skirt

Net is cheap to buy and available in a wide range of colors. This is easy to make but you may require some adult help with gathering the fabric.

You will need:
2yds of 54in wide net
1yd of $2^1/2$in wide ribbon
needle and thread
elastic

172

1 Fold the net in half lengthways, then in half again, so you have four layers.

2 Stitch through the double fold of fabric, about $1/2$in from the fold, with a running stitch.

3 Pull up the thread, to gather the fabric, until the gathered edge measures 1yd.

4 Fold the ribbon in half lengthways and place over the gathered edge. Pin in place, then stitch firmly through all layers, close to the edge of the ribbon.

5 Cut a piece of elastic long enough to go around your waist. Pin a safety-pin at the end of the elastic and use this to help thread it through the ribbon. Stitch the ends of the elastic and ribbon together. Cut through the folds on the bottom edge.

Fairy wand

Cut two star shapes from thick cardboard and tape back to back, with the end of a stick in between. Paint the stars and the stick, adding glitter for sparkle and gluing on some jewels. Tie lengths of ribbon around the top of the stick.

Fairy wings

These require adult help, particularly when cutting and bending wire into shape. Use millinery wire or two coat hangers with the hooks cut off. Make sure you cover the sharp ends of the wire with plenty of tape. To join the two wings, any fabric will do but something shiny or metallic, such as silver lamé, looks best.

You will need:
1.8yds medium gauge wire
pair of sheer pantyhose
sticky tape
scraps of silver fabric
needle and thread
28in narrow elastic
newspaper
pots of fabric paints
paintbrush
tubes of glittery and neon
fabric paints

1 Cut the wire into two equal lengths and, using the wings pictured here as a guide, bend into wing shapes. Join the ends of the wire by binding them with sticky tape.

2 Cut the legs off a pair of pantyhose and push one wing into each leg. Stitch the cut edges together at the point where the ends are joined.

3 Cut two pieces of fabric, each measuring 5in x 3¹/₂in. Fold in the edges by about ¹/₂in all round. Place one of the fabric pieces with the two short ends covering the joins in the wire and the cut edges of the pantyhose. Stitch in place. Do the same with the other piece of fabric, on the other side of the wings.

4 Cut two 14in lengths of elastic and stitch to the fabric, level with the inside edges of the wings, to form loops to slip over your shoulders.

5 Place the wings on a thick pile of newspaper and paint, using fabric paints, diluted with an equal amount of water. For the best effect, using two or three colors. Leave to dry – for about 2 hours.

173

6 Using glittery and neon fabric paints, squeeze squiggly patterns over the wings. Leave to dry, flat, overnight.

Customized T-shirts

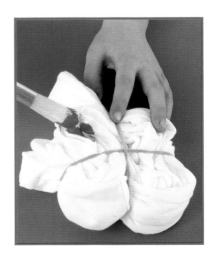

Transform a plain white vest into an explosion of color and pattern with brilliant tie-dye.

Swirly vest

This is a great way to smarten up an old vest! If you are dyeing a new vest, you will need to wash it first, or the dye may not soak into the fabric.

You will need:
cotton vest
elastic bands
cold water dyes in blue,
red and yellow
rubber gloves
thick paintbrush

1 Wash your vest, wring out most of the water but leave it damp.

2 For a swirly effect, lay the vest flat, pinch the center with your finger and thumb, and twist into a spiral. Secure the bundle with two elastic bands, dividing it into four sections.

3 Dissolve the dye powder in warm water, adding fixative and salt according to the packet instructions. Make up the three different colors separately.

4 Protect your work surface with plastic bags and your hands with rubber gloves. Use the paintbrush to apply dye to the vest, painting each section a different color. To achieve a similar effect to the vest on this page, paint two opposite quarters blue, one yellow, and one red. Make sure the fabric is well saturated with dye.

5 Place the vest in a plastic bag, seal, and leave overnight.

6 Remove the vest from the bag and rinse in cold water until the water runs clear, then remove the elastic bands. Then wash the vest in hot, soapy water, rinse, and dry.

Crafty tips
• You could dye other items of clothing, too – cotton underwear, socks or pants, for example.
• When buying dyes, ask a assistant for advice. You will need cold water dyes that are suitable for cotton fabrics and are permanent (so they won't wash out). You will probably need to use a special dye fixative and some salt, too. Check the instructions in the pack of dye before you start.

Sunburst vest

To achieve a sunburst or target effect, place the vest on a flat surface, pinch the center and lift. Add elastic bands at intervals, dividing the vest into three or more sections, and dye each section a different color.

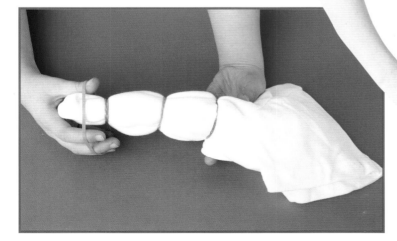

Prehistoric Pranks

This is the easiest costume to make, as it requires no sewing, just a bit of artful arranging!

Caveman club

This primitive weapon looks heavy but is very lightweight – but it's just for decoration, so don't be tempted to hit anyone over the head with it!

You will need:
cardboard tube
empty plastic bottle
sticky tape
newspapers
white craft glue
paintbrush
acrylic paints

1 Place the cardboard tube over the neck of the bottle, and tape firmly in place.

2 Roll up a sheet of newspaper, wrap it around the bottle, and tape in place.

3 Pour some glue into a plastic cup or a jelly jar and add an equal amount of water. Stir well and brush the mixture all over the club, then apply pieces of newspaper, torn into strips. Build up about four layers of paper and glue in this way, and leave to dry.

4 Paint the finished club with a layer of white paint, leave to dry, then paint it brown.

Animal skin tunic

This costume is produced without any sewing – and fits most sizes! From a piece of animal print fabric measuring 64in x 34in, cut a strip 4in wide from one long side, to make a sash. Fold the remaining piece in half across its width and cut along the fold for 20in. Place the fabric with the uncut 10in on your shoulder, wrap the fabric around your body, and tie the sash around your waist to hold it all in place.

Prehistoric hair

If you have short hair, dampen it slightly with water, then rub hair gel into it, particularly near the roots. Use your fingers to ruffle and spike the strands, making it look as spiky and tangled as possible. Tie a strip of fabric around your head. If you have long hair, tie it in a pony tail on top of your head. Wind a strip of fabric round and round the ponytail to make it stick up.

Ancient accessories

If you have any spare fabric, cut it into strips, about 2in wide, and wrap these around your feet. You could wrap them around your wrists or upper arms, too, or use one to create a headband.

Bags of Ideas

Here are some bags that are stylish as well as practical, and just require the most basic of sewing skills

Bear bag

Made from fleece and felt, which do not fray, this is easy to stitch.

You will need:
purple fleece fabric, at least
20in x 8in
colored felt
needle and thread
24in cord
button

1 Cut two pieces of fleece, each measuring 10in x 8in.

2 Cut the bear shape from brown felt and stitch in place on one of the pieces of fleece, using a contrasting colored thread and running stitch.

3 Cut other details from felt and stitch in place, oversewing the edges neatly.

4 Place the two pieces of fleece together, with the bear motif inside. Stitch the sides and base together, 1/2in from the edges. Turn under 3/4in at the top edge, to form a hem, and stitch in place.

5 Stitch the two ends of the cord to the side seams on the inside of the bag.

Snail bag

This is made in exactly the same way as the bear bag. Cut the pieces from felt, using the colors shown or your own choice of colors. Or use your imagination to create your own colorful motifs.

Spiral bag

Cut strips of felt, $1/2$in wide and about 3in long. Place four strips of different colors on top of each other and roll up tightly. Hold in place with a pin and stitch securely. Use to decorate a fleece bag, stitching them firmly in place along the hem line.

Jeans bag

Cut the legs off a pair of jeans, leaving the top part to make your bag. Turn this part inside out and stitch the cut edges together, to form the base of the bag. Cut a strip from the inside leg seam of each leg, cutting about $3/4$in on either side of the seam. Join the two pieces, then fold in the raw edges and stitch, to form a strap. Stitch each end of the strap to the bag.

Desert Island Dreams

Even on a dull day, put on this costume and you will be transported to a tropical island. And all you need is some crêpe paper, tissue, fabric scraps, and a few plastic bags!

Hula hula costume

Use your own choice of colors – crêpe paper is available in lots of bright colors – the brighter the better!

You will need:
crêpe paper, 20in wide, in green, pink, yellow and orange
strip of fabric, 1.4yds x 4^{1}/2in
needle and thread

1 Cut two 24in lengths of each color of crêpe paper. This will be the length of the finished skirt.

2 Place the paper in two piles, each containing one sheet of each color. Place the piles side by side, with one of the short edges uppermost.

3 Mark the center point of the strip of fabric. Fold in the two long edges. Fold in half lengthways and place over the paper, to form a waistband. The center point of the fabric should line up with the division between the two piles of paper. Stitch the waistband in place, through all thicknesses, so the paper is securely trapped inside the folded fabric.

4 Now cut the paper into strips, starting at the bottom edge and cutting toward the waistband.

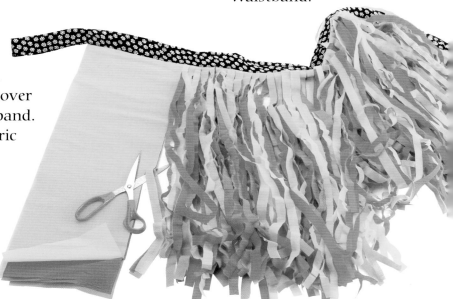

Floral hair

Some artificial flowers, stitched to a hair slide, will help to dress up your hair.

Hula hula garland

Cut strips measuring 4½in wide from a plastic carrier bag and from colored tissue paper. For a short garland, these strips should be about 32in long and for a long garland, about 1yd. Choose the most colorful, shiny plastic bag you can find and, if it's not big enough, you can cut several strips and join them together.

To make the garland, sandwich two or three strips of tissue paper between two strips of plastic. Stitch up the center, through all layers, then join the two ends. Snip either side of the stitching, into a fringe, then crumple and ruffle the garland in your hands.

Clips and Pins

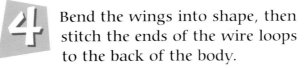

For a perfect finishing touch, and the chance to really show off your creative skills, make a brooch or a hair slide.

Butterfly brooch

This is made from old pantyhose! Use sheer pantyhose in any color you like. Ask an adult for help with cutting and bending wire.

You will need:
20in of medium gauge wire
1 pair of pantyhose
$3^1/2$in plastic-coated wire
beads
tubes of fabric paint
glitter
brooch pin

1 Cut the medium gauge wire into four equal lengths and bend each one into a loop, twisting the ends together, to form the wings.

2 Cut across the leg of the pantyhose at $3^1/2$in intervals. Stretch one of these pieces over each of the wire loops, gathering the cut ends together, and stitching in place where the ends of the wire are twisted together.

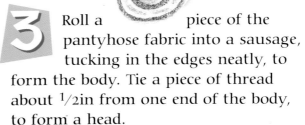

3 Roll a   piece of the pantyhose fabric into a sausage, tucking in the edges neatly, to form the body. Tie a piece of thread about $1/2$in from one end of the body, to form a head.

4 Bend the wings into shape, then stitch the ends of the wire loops to the back of the body.

5 Bend the plastic-coated wire in half and stitch to the back of the head. Thread a bead on to each end of the wire and bend the wire over the beads to hold them in place.

6 Decorate the body and wings with fabric paint, squeezed straight from the tube. You could use glittery fabric paints, or a plain color sprinkled with fine glitter in a variety of different colors. Leave to dry, preferably overnight.

7 Stitch a brooch pin to the back of the butterfly.

Hair combs

Wind a 14in length of narrow ribbon between the teeth and around the top of a plain plastic hair comb. Repeat with a second color of ribbon. Leave it like this, or glue on tiny fabric flowers, using a dot of fabric glue.

183

Floral band

Wind a long length of narrow ribbon round and round a plain hair band. Tuck small sprigs of artificial flowers under the ribbon as you go. As long as you wind the ribbon really tightly, it will hold the flower stems in place.

Fantastic Feathers

Native American head-dresses are the inspiration for this feathered headgear, which is colorful and as much fun to make as it is to wear.

Feather head-dress

You will really feel like a big chief when you wear this magnificent creation! It requires large and small feathers, available in craft stores. Red, yellow, and green create an authentic effect but you could choose your own color combination.

You will need:
red corrugated cardboard
stapler
10 small green feathers
10 small red feathers
7 long feathers
10 small blue feathers
1 small yellow feather
11in red marabou feather trim
14in of $1/2$in elastic

1 Cut a circle with a diameter of 12in from corrugated cardboard. Cut this in half, then cut a 2in strip from each half (and save these to make a head band).

2 Staple the green feathers, evenly spaced, to the inside of one of the cardboard pieces, along the curved edge. Staple the red feathers in between.

3 Staple the long feathers, evenly spaced, on top of the red and green ones.

4 Because the staples will now show at the front, staple the blue feathers to the front of the cardboard, to hide them. Staple a yellow feather in the center and staple the marabou trim along the bottom edge.

5 At the back of the cardboard, staple the ends of the elastic to either side, then glue the second piece of cardboard over the back, to hide the ends of the feathers and the staples.

Feather head band

Cut a strip of corrugated cardboard 19in long and 2in wide (or join the two pieces you have left over from making the headdress). Join the two ends with two 4in pieces of elastic, stapled to the cardboard. Glue on paper cut-outs, then push feathers into the top of the band.

Hair braid

Cut three 36in lengths of cotton yarn or embroidery floss, fold in half, and tie a knot, to create a loop. Braid the strands and, when you get to the ends, thread on some beads and tie on a feather. The loop can be attached to a hair slide or an elastic band.

Novelty Necklaces

Look around for fun things to thread on to necklaces, from plastic fruit to clothespins!

Clothespin necklace

Tiny clothespins are available from stationery stores. Thread string through the hole in each pin, adding beads if you like.

Fruity necklace

This is made from plastic fruits that were filled with candy. Empty out the candies and thread the fruits on to a length of string. You should be able to stick a needle through the plastic. Thread beads in between each fruit, then knot the ends of the string.

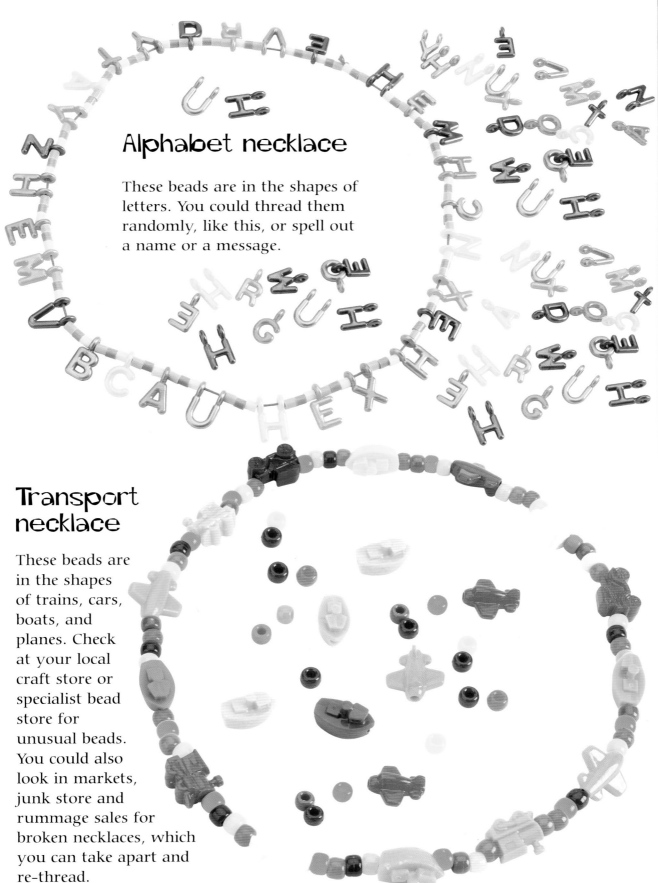

Alphabet necklace

These beads are in the shapes of letters. You could thread them randomly, like this, or spell out a name or a message.

Transport necklace

These beads are in the shapes of trains, cars, boats, and planes. Check at your local craft store or specialist bead store for unusual beads. You could also look in markets, junk store and rummage sales for broken necklaces, which you can take apart and re-thread.

Royal Regalia

If you're dressing up as a king, a queen, a prince, or princess, these accessories will add just the right finishing touches!

Crown

Papier mâché forms a thick, solid yet lightweight base for a crown that you can paint and decorate in any way you like.

You will need:
corrugated cardboard
sticky tape
white craft glue
paintbrush
newspapers
acrylic paints
fake jewels

1 Cut a strip of corrugated cardboard 24in x 9in. Cut out triangular notches along one of the long sides. Join the ends, to form a crown. Check that it fits on your head. It should be very loose at this stage, as it will fit more tightly once it has been covered with several layers of paper and paint.

2 Cut a second strip of cardboard, 24in x 2in, and wrap this around the base of the crown, taping it firmly in place.

3 Dilute the glue with an equal amount of water and brush the mixture all over the crown, then apply pieces of newspaper, torn into strips. Build up about four layers of paper and glue in this way, and leave to dry.

4 Paint the finished crown with a layer of white paint, leave to dry, then paint it gold. Stick a fake jewel to each point of the crown.

Hand mirror

You can buy mirror board in art stores. It is a very glossy, silver-coated cardboard with a mirror-like surface, and much safer than using a real mirror, which could get broken.

You will need:
cardboard
mirror board
sticky tape
white craft glue
paintbrush
newspapers
acrylic paints
glitter glue
fake jewels

1 Draw an oval shape on a piece of cardboard, with a smaller oval in the center. Add a handle. Cut this shape out, then draw around its outline on another piece of cardboard, and cut this shape out.

2 Cut a piece of mirror board, slightly larger than the small oval hole. Tape it behind the hole, then tape the second cardboard piece behind it.

3 Dilute the glue with an equal amount of water and brush the mixture all over the frame, back and front, then apply pieces of newspaper, torn into strips. Try not to get glue on the surface of the mirror board. Build up about four layers of paper and glue and leave to dry.

4 Paint the finished frame with a layer of white paint, leave to dry, then paint it gold.

5 Squeeze a thin line of glitter glue around the inner edge of the frame and add tiny gems whole the glue is still wet. Stick on more jewels using small blobs of glitter glue. Leave to dry.

Beads and Pins

Thread small glass beads on elastic to make the simplest bracelets – and on to safety pins for a set of stylish jewelry. For something bolder, make your own beads from colored paper!

Paper beads

For a different effect, or if you do not have sheets of colored paper, use any scraps of paper you have available. You could use old letters or documents, for example, or pages cut from magazines.

You will need:
sheets of colored paper
knitting needle or stick
glue stick or
double-sided sticky tape

1 Cut strips along the length of the paper. The strips can be straight, or they can be tapered, with one end wider than the other.

2 Roll a strip around a knitting needle or stick, sticking the end down with a glue stick or double-sided tape.

3 Thread your home-made beads on to lengths of string, knotting the ends.

Friendship bracelets

Thread small glass or plastic beads on to narrow elastic. You can buy really thin, strong elastic specially designed for jewelry-making, from craft stores. Knot the ends of the elastic firmly, slipping the knot inside one of the beads.

Make bracelets from beads of all one color and size, or mix colors and shapes, whichever you prefer.

Safety pin jewelry

Thread glass beads on to safety pins. To make a bracelet, thread one piece of cord elastic through the loops at one ends of the pins and another piece of elastic through the holes at the other ends of the pins. Add a bead in between each pin. Knot the ends of the elastic together.

To make a necklace, thread a length of string or cord through the pins, with beads in between.

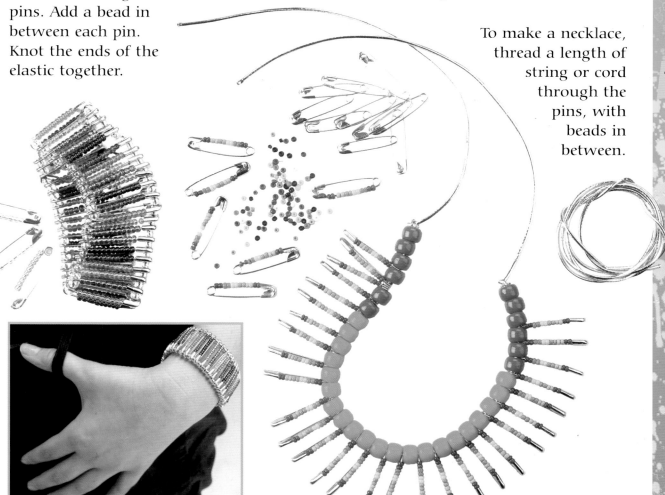

Brilliant Beads

Beads are available in all shapes, sizes, and colors, so have a go at making some fabulous jewelry for yourself or as a gift for a friend.

Bead brooch

Small beads are stitched to a fabric backing. It's fiddly but quite easy to do, and you can choose your own color combinations – or even make up your own design.

You will need:
small scrap of interfacing
or stiff fabric
pen
beads
needle and thread
thin cardboard
fabric glue
felt
brooch pin

1 Draw a 1¹/₂in square on the interfacing, then draw your design within the square.

2 Starting at the center, sew beads to the fabric, keeping them close together and filling the shapes you have drawn.

3 When the design is covered with beads, trim the edges, leaving a small margin of fabric all round the square, and fold this to the back.

4 Cut a 1¹/₂in square of cardboard and glue to the back of the fabric, then fold the edges of fabric over and stick them in place.

5 Cut a 1¹/₂in square of felt and place this over the back of the fabric, to cover all the stitching. You can glue the felt in place, using fabric glue, or stitch it round the edges. Finally, stitch a brooch pin to the center of the felt.

Beaded bracelet

Thread small glass beads on to a long length of wire, then wind round and round a plain plastic bracelet. If you haven't got a suitable bracelet, could use the cardboard ring from the center of a roll of sticky tape.

Bead necklaces

Thread beads into strings as long as you like. Use strong thread, which you can buy from specialist bead stores, or try using dental floss, which is very strong and easy to knot. Tie the ends of the thread to the loops of a metal necklace fastening.

Outdoor Fun

Contents

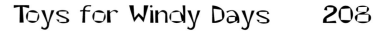

Introduction

When the weather is fine, it is great to get outdoors and enjoy the sunshine. You may want to plant or you may want to play. Whatever you like doing, *Outdoor Fun* is packed with ideas to help you make the most of life in the backyard!

If you are lucky enough to have access to a backyard, you may be allowed your own space: perhaps a quiet corner where you can plant some flowers or herbs, or make a den? It may be, however, that your only outdoor space is a windowsill or balcony – but you can still test out your green thumb by planting something in a pot or trough and watching it grow!

And when you are out and about in the park or countryside, or by the sea, collect stuff like pebbles, shells, twigs, and driftwood so that, on a rainy afternoon, you can turn them into something – a wind chime,

maybe, or a paperweight. Check out *Outdoor Fun* for some great projects using found objects.

Tools and materials

You may find what you need in the garage, or perhaps an adult can help you collect some stuff together. For planting projects, flower pots are useful, though you may be able to use other things as planting containers: baskets lined with plastic, yogurt tubs, an old plastic bucket? Compost, gravel, and broken clay pots are useful for planting cuttings and seeds. And, of course, you will need plants. Bedding plants, available from late spring, are inexpensive – but packets of seeds are even cheaper!

Get yourself a big cardboard box and try to collect together some or all of the following items, in order to make the projects on the following pages: string, nylon thread, peanuts, aluminum foil, acrylic paints and brushes, colored paper, wooden kebab sticks, popsicle sticks, bamboo poles, scissors, a glue stick, sand, fabric paints, drinking straws, a permanent marker pen, wire coat hangers, fine wire, mosaic tiles and waterproof tile adhesive, rags, fabric scraps, canvas or calico fabric, ribbons, straw, and some empty paint cans.

Easy to make

Most projects are simple and straightforward - just follow the instructions and you won't go far wrong! Sometimes you may wish to change things - and that's fine! If the instructions say "plant pansies" and all you have are some geraniums, then plant the geraniums instead!

You may occasionally need the help of an adult - or at least an adult's permission if, for example, you wish to pick some flowers from the yard!

Brilliant Containers

Pot plants don't have to live in plant pots! Be inventive with your choice of containers! Almost anything will do. Look around the house and see what you can find.

Things you need to know

Compost
To be healthy, a container-grown plant should be planted in potting compost, not soil from the backyard, and the container should have adequate drainage. You can buy potting compost in small bags from garden centers and hardware store.

Water
Most plant pots have holes in the base for water to drain out. If your container does not have holes, be sure to put a good layer of gravel in the base before adding your compost, to allow excess water to drain away from the plant's roots. Water your plant frequently. Do not allow the compost to dry out, but do not over-water either. The compost should be damp.

Suitable plants
Bedding plants are not very expensive. Choose from those labeled as being suitable for window boxes, containers, and hanging baskets. Pansies, primulas, and petunias are all easily available and suitable for small containers. For a medium-sized container, you could also choose geraniums or chrysanthemums.

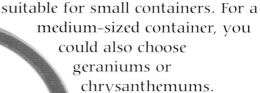

Truck container

Here, a plastic toy truck has been planted with pansies. What a great idea to brighten up the yard!

You will need:
suitable container
gravel, pebbles, or broken clay pots
potting compost
small bedding plants

1 Put a layer of gravel, pebbles, or broken clay pots in the base of your container. Then add compost, about two-thirds full.

2 Place the plants on top and add a little more compost to fill any gaps, pressing it down lightly with your fingertips.

3 Add water until the compost is moist.

Naturally Crafty

You may not find a bundle of twigs particularly inspiring – but you'd be surprised what you can make! Collect fallen twigs from the park for a star decoration, or long vine stems from your own backyard for a wreath. On your next trip to the seaside, search the shoreline for driftwood and, while you're at it, see if you can find some seashells. Not any old shells but ones with holes in, so they can be transformed into a pretty outdoor mobile.

Crafty tips
Suitable stems for this project include those from Virginia creeper, Boston ivy, some honeysuckles, or a grape vine. Ask a grown-up to help you. The best time to cut the stems is in the fall, after the leaves have dropped off.

Wreath

Some people like to hang a decorated wreath on their front door at Christmas time. But a simple, undecorated wreath makes an attractive decoration any time of the year. You could even tie on a bunch of dried lavender, to make a scented wreath! But first, you will need to collect some long, flexible stems from a vine or climbing shrub – about 12-15 stems.

1 Start with a long stem, bending it round into a circle and twisting the ends around the circle until they stay in place.

2 Take a second stem, push the thicker end into a gap where you have twisted the ends of the first piece, then wind it round and round the circle, tucking the end into a gap.

3 Add a third stem, then a fourth, and as many more stems as you like.

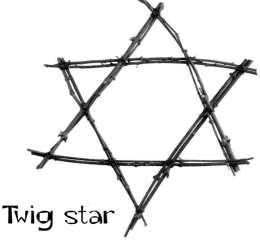

To make a string of peanuts

Simply thread a large darning needle with string and thread peanuts in their shells on to the string, just as if you were making a necklace. Knot the ends so the peanuts do not slide off! Simply tie to a tree for the birds to eat.

Twig star

Choose three twigs of similar lengths, and bind the ends together with fine wire to make a triangle. Make another triangle, place one on top of the other, and bind together where they overlap.

Shell wind chime

You will need:
assortment of shells, with holes
nylon thread
twig or small piece of driftwood
string

1 Cut short lengths of thread and tie firmly on to shells. Tie the other end of each piece to the twig or driftwood.

2 Cut more short lengths of thread, tie one end to the bottom of the first shell, then add another shell. Tie on more shells, until you are pleased with the arrangement. Make sure they are quite close together so they will knock into each other when the wind blows.

3 Tie a length of string to each end of the stick and hang up your shell wind chime in the house or yard, where it will catch the breeze.

Edible Plants from Seed

Growing things to eat can be magic! You plant your seeds, then you stare at the bare earth for days, thinking nothing will happen. Suddenly tiny green shoots poke through – and before you know it you have a crop of plants!

Parsley pot

You will need
parsley pot or large flower pot
gravel, pebbles, or broken clay pots
seed compost
parsley seeds

Parsley seeds are tiny and slow to sprout, so you have to be patient. If you can, sow them in a parsley pot – a large flower pot with several planting holes on the sides. Keep parsley well watered and cut it as often as you like – chop it up and add it to vegetables, scrambled eggs, pies, sandwiches, almost any savory food! And every week or so throughout the summer, keep sowing more seed in your pot, so your supply never runs out!

1 Place a layer of gravel, pebbles, or broken clay pots in the base of the pot, then fill with compost to within about 1 inch of the rim.

2 Sprinkle the surface of the compost with a thin layer of seeds, then add a little more compost – just enough to cover the seeds lightly.

3 Water until the compost is damp.

Nasturtiums

These are one of the easiest plants to grow from seed. The seeds are larger than most, and easy to handle. Push three or four into a pot of compost in late spring, sprinkle with water, and you should see shoots appearing in a few days.

As the plants grow, gently push a few sticks into the soil to give support to the climbing stems. With three sticks tied together at the top, you can make a nasturtium wigwam.

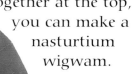

Bottle top bird scarers

To protect newly sprouted seeds and small plants from being eaten by birds, make a bird scarer. Attach pieces of aluminum foil to a length of string suspended just above the young plants.

203

Or why not grow a nasturtium seed in a plastic bottle? Before planting, use a skewer to make a few drainage holes in the base of the bottle, add a layer of gravel to help drainage, then fill with compost.

Water your plants daily and by late summer, you should have mass of leaves and red, orange, and yellow flowers. Both leaves and flowers are edible – add them to salads for a peppery flavor.

Painted Pebbles

The next time you go to the beach, look out for some nice, round pebbles to paint. Paint one to make a paperweight, or a whole pocketful to make a snake!

You will need:
round, flat pebbles
acrylic paints
soft paintbrush

Pebble Paperweight

1 Firstly, paint your pebble white. You will have to paint one side, then leave it to dry before painting the other side.

2 Now use bright colors to paint a design. The shape of the pebble may suggest what kind of decoration to choose: maybe a flower or a fish?

Crafty tip
Acrylic paints give a hard-wearing finish, but for added protection why not paint your finished pebbles with a coat of water-based varnish?

Pebble snake

1 Paint pebbles white, as before. Leave to dry.

2 Paint each pebble the same, plain color, then add the squiggles. Add a spot to one pebble as the snake's eye.

3 Arrange pebbles in a wiggly line, with the largest as the snake's head, with progressively smaller pebbles towards the tail.

Sandcastle flags

Playing with sand is fun, whether you are at the beach or in the sandpit. And what better way to adorn a sandcastle than with a selection of home-made paper flags?

To make paper flags

You will need:
selection of colored paper scraps
felt pens
glue stick
scissors
wooden kebab sticks

1 For the main part of each flag, cut a rectangle measuring 5 x 3 inches. Decorate the flags with felt pens or by gluing on paper cut-outs.

2 Apply a little glue to one of the short edges, place the stick on top, and roll the paper round the stick.

Sand play
If you haven't got a bucket and spade, improvise with things you may have in the kitchen. Use a sieve or colander for sifting sand, wooden or plastic spoons and forks for scooping and scraping, and plastic cups for making sand pies!

205

Garden Parties

On sunny summer days, if you are lucky enough to have a suitable space to play outside, invite your friends round, create a hide-away in the backyard and be prepared for some fun and adventure!

To make a wigwam

You will need:
3 yards of calico,
approximately 60 inches wide
tape measure
scissors
fabric paints and paintbrush
needle and strong thread
four bamboo poles, approximately 6 feet long
string or cord

1 Cut the calico into four equal pieces, each measuring 60 x 27 inches. Fold one piece in half lengthwise and draw a line from the folded corner at one end to the opposite corner at the other end. Cut along this line, to make a tall triangle. Repeat with the other three pieces.

2 Lay the pieces out flat on a surface covered with plenty of newspaper, draw design outlines in pencil, then fill in with fabric paint. Leave to dry.

3 Stitch the triangles together, down their long sides, to make a kind of pyramid. When joining the last two edges, only stitch for about 20 inches, leaving an opening so you can get in and out of your tent.

4 Stick the bottom ends of the bamboo poles in the ground, in a square formation, about 2 feet apart. Tie the top ends together, leaving the long ends of the string or cord dangling. Now slip the fabric over the poles and wind the ends of the string round and round the top, securing the fabric to the poles.

207

To make a den

If you have a large piece of fabric, an old sheet or blanket, you can make an "instant" den without any sewing or painting. Simply drape the fabric over a laundry line, weighting the edges with stones, or tie it between low tree branches, bushes, or a wall or fence.

Toys for Windy Days

A paper windmill is easy to make: stick it in the sand at the beach, or in a flower pot in your yard and watch it spin when the wind blows. A wind sock will show you the direction of the wind – and it's great fun to run along holding the stick, with the colorful ribbon streamers trailing behind you!

To make a windmill

You will need:
tracing paper
thin cardboard
scissors
glass-headed pin
2 plastic drinking straws
cork

B

A

1 Trace off the petal shape from this page and use it as a template to cut seven petal shapes from thin cardboard.

2 Stick the pin through all the cardboard petals at point A.

3 Cut a ¹/₂ inch length from one of the straws and place it on the pin. Then stick the pin through all petals at point B.

4 Cut another short length from the straw and place it on the pin. Stick the pin point through the top of the other straw, then cut off a small piece of the cork and stick it on the pin point.

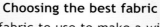

To make a wind sock

You will need:
fabric (see box on right)
scissors
needle and sewing thread
wire
ribbons
string or cord
small metal ring
metal spinner
stick

1 Cut a rectangle of fabric measuring $13^1/2$ inches. Stitch the two short ends together, to make a cylinder. Then turn under about $1/2$ inch at each end, to form a hem, and stitch.

2 Push a length of wire into one of the hems, joining the ends of the wire by twisting them together.

3 Cut ribbons into 16 inches lengths and stitch to the other hem.

Choosing the best fabric
The best fabric to use to make a wind sock is parachute nylon, available from speciality kite shops, but you could use acetate lining fabric or another lightweight fabric.

4 Cut three $13^1/2$ inches lengths of string or cord. Make three holes in the top hem, below the wire, and thread the strings through these holes, tying tightly. Thread the other ends of the three strings through the metal ring and tie firmly, then attach the ring to the spinner.

Crafty tips
Metal spinners can be bought from kite shops or stores selling jewelry-making components. The spinner will help to prevent strings getting tangled. If, however, you do not have a spinner, you can tie the strings directly to the top of the stick.

209

5 Tie a short length of string to the other end of the spinner and tie the string securely to the stick.

Make a Herb Pot

Most herbs can be cultivated indoors on a windowsill for an all-year-round supply. But in summer, they will thrive outdoors in sunny conditions, so why not plant up a selection in a large container?

You will need:
large terra-cotta bowl or similar container
gravel, pebbles, or broken
clay pots
potting compost
selection of small herb plants

1 Put gravel, pebbles, or broken clay pots in the base of your container, then fill about two-thirds full with compost.

2 Arrange the herbs on top of the compost. Try to make a balanced arrangement, with the tallest plants such as rosemary, chives, or sage in the center and lower growing types such as parsley, marjoram, and oregano around the edges. Thyme, which is very low growing, will tumble over the rim of the pot. Leave gaps between the plants.

3 Keep your herb pot well watered and the plants will grow and thrive and fill the gaps until you have a lovely, scented mass of greenery.

Crafty tips
Keep trimming the plants and use the bits you cut off in cooking.

Popsicle stick plant labels

Every time you have an ice popsicle, save the stick. These flat wooden sticks are ideal for labeling plants – especially seeds and bulbs which, once you have put them in the ground, you might easily forget!

To make plant labels

You will need:
popsicle sticks
acrylic paints
paintbrush
permanent marker pen

1 Use paints to decorate one side of each stick with stripes, spots, or other patterns.

2 Using the marker pen, write information about the seeds, bulbs, or cuttings you have planted, such as the name and date of planting, on the other side.

Topiary Tricks

Topiary is the art of trimming hedges and shrubs into decorative shapes and a lot of skill is required. But here are two ideas that you can try yourself, to make shapes that look a bit like topiary hedges but with a bit of cheating!

You will need:
large flower pot
gravel, pebbles or broken clay pots
potting compost
two wire coat hangers
fine wire
one or more ivy plants

To make an ivy ball

1 Put gravel, pebbles, or broken clay pots in the base of your flower pot, then fill about two-thirds full with compost.

2 Bend the coat hangers by holding the center of the bar in one hand and the hook in the other, and pulling until it forms a diamond shape. Pull the hooks straight, to form the stem (ask a grown-up to help). Slot the two coat hangers together to form a cube shape. Use small lengths of fine wire to bind the two together at the top and bind the twisted ends together to form the "tail."

3 Push the "tail" into the center of the pot. Plant the ivy and add a bit more compost, to come to within 1 inch of the rim of the pot.

4 Twist the ivy around the wire. As it grows, help to guide it around the wire.

How to make a rosemary ball

You will need:
large flower pot
gravel, pebbles, or broken
clay pots
potting compost
rosemary plant
scissors

1 Put a layer of gravel, pebbles, or broken clay pots in the base of your pot. Then add compost, about two-thirds full. Add your rosemary plant and a little more compost.

2 With scissors, cut off lower stems, then trim ends of upper stems, to make a rough ball shape. As the rosemary grows, give it a "haircut" with your scissors every few weeks to keep it in shape.

Marvelous Mosaics

Decorative mosaics have been around for thousands of years. If you make your own, they can't be guaranteed to last that long, but if you are careful, they should withstand all kinds of weather.

Safety

This is a project that needs some adult help. Before you start, unless you wish to use only whole tiles, you will need to ask a grown-up to break the tiles into small pieces. This is best done with a special tool called a tile nipper. After the tiles have been cut, they should be washed to remove any small splinters of glass, and you should wear gloves when you are handling them, as the edges are likely to be sharp.

To make a mosaic pot

You will need:
spatula
waterproof tile adhesive and grout
terra-cotta flower pot
vitreous mosaic tiles
rags

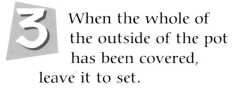

1 Using the spatula, spread a thick layer of tile grout over the surface of the pot.

2 Press pieces of mosaic tile into the grout, leaving small gaps between each piece.

3 When the whole of the outside of the pot has been covered, leave it to set.

4 Using the spatula again, add more tile grout, pressing it into the gaps between the tiles. With a damp rag, wipe away any excess grout. Leave to set.

5 Use a dry rag to remove any remaining grout from the surface of the tiles.

To make a mosaic number tile

Start with a square of thick plywood or a large ceramic tile. Draw a number on the surface, using a waterproof marker pen. Spread tile grout in the area where you have drawn the number and fill with pieces of tile in your chosen color. Then use whole, unbroken mosaic tiles all round the edge, for a neat border. Spread tile grout over the remaining area and fill in the background with pieces of tile. Leave to dry, then fill in gaps between tiles with more grout, wiping away excess with a damp cloth.

Crafty tips
To stick down the pieces of mosaic and fill in the gaps between, use a combined waterproof tile grout and adhesive, which is available ready mixed in a plastic tub as a thick white paste. It is advizable to wear gloves when handling this adhesive.

Early Daffodils

Fall is the time when gardeners plant spring bulbs. Daffodil, crocus, and hyacinth bulbs, buried under the soil in late September and October, will magically push up shoots in early spring and burst into a blaze of color. But here's a way to cheat nature and produce spring blossoms in plenty of time for Christmas!

You will need:
gravel
colander
3 paper white narcissus bulbs
glass container

1 Wash the gravel. Tip it into a colander and wash with plenty of cold running water, until the water runs clear.

2 Carefully fill your glass container with the clean gravel, to within about 1 1/2 inches of the rim. Place the bulbs, root side down, on top of the gravel.

3 Add a little more gravel, to help support the bulbs, then pour in water until it is level with the base of the bulbs.

4 Place the container on a sunny windowsill and watch your bulbs grow. Within days, green shoots should appear from the tops of the bulbs and you will soon see the white roots pushing their way down through the gravel. If you are lucky, your bulbs will produce flowers in a matter of weeks!

Plant an all-seasons window box

Not everyone has a backyard – but most of us have a windowsill. Plant up a window box using heathers and conifers and they should brighten up your view all year long.

You will need:
small trough or similar container
gravel, pebbles, or broken clay pots
potting compost
small conifers
heathers
one or more ivy plants

1 Put gravel, pebbles, or broken clay pots in the base of your trough, then fill about two-thirds full with compost.

2 Arrange the conifers and heathers on top of the compost. Try to make a balanced arrangement. In a very small trough, you could put a conifer in the center, and a heather either side. In a larger container, you might have room for three conifers, with heathers in between.

3 If you add ivy to the front of the arrangement, as it grows it will trail down over the trough.

4 Fill in the gaps between the plants with more compost, pressing it down firmly with your hands. Water the trough and continue to water daily, or as often as you need to, to keep the compost moist but not too wet.

217

Window box scarecrow

You will need:
2 sticks
string or raffia
fabric scraps or
doll's clothes
straw
waterproof marker pen

1 Cross the sticks at right angles and tie firmly together with string or raffia.

2 Squeeze some straw into ball and place in the center of a circle of fabric. Gather fabric around the straw and place on top of one of the sticks, to form a head. Tie in place and draw on a face with waterproof marker pen.

3 Stuff doll's clothes with straw – or cut and stitch fabric into a simple tunic shape – and push the sticks through the neck and arms. Make sure there is some straw sticking out of the sleeves for an authentic look!

Pressed Flowers

Here's a way to preserve flower heads, petals, and leaves collected from the yard, and use them to decorate a card and a bookmark.

To press flowers

You will need:
heavy book
blotting paper or paper kitchen towels
flowers and leaves (see Crafty tip)

1 Open out the book and place a sheet of blotting paper or kitchen paper on one page. Arrange flower heads, petals, and leaves over the paper, leaving spaces in between.

Crafty tip
Pick flowers at the end of a dry day. The best types to press are flat flower heads or separate petals. You can also press leaves and stems. Avoid very fat, fleshy flowers, berries, and seed pods as these do not dry out successfully and tend to rot and go brown.

2 Place a second piece of paper on top, taking care not to dislodge the flowers and leaves. Close the book. Place it flat with several more books on top and leave for two or three weeks.

3 Check to see if your flowers and leaves have dried out. Open up the book carefully and peel the petals and leaves from the paper. If they are stuck they may not be dry enough and you should leave them for a week or two longer. If, however, they are dry and papery, they are ready to be used.

To make a pressed flower bookmark

You will need:
pressed flowers and leaves
thin cardboard
glue stick
clear self-adhesive plastic film
hole punch
ribbon

1 Arrange pressed flowers and leaves on a strip of thin cardboard. To hold them in place, use a tiny dab of glue.

2 Cut a piece of self-adhesive film about 1 inch larger all round than the cardboard. Peel off the backing paper and place the decorated cardboard face down centrally on the sticky side of the film. Trim off any excess film.

3 Punch a hole at the bottom of the bookmark and thread the ribbon through.

To make a pressed flower card

Fold a rectangle of thin cardboard in half. Arrange flowers and leaves on the front and stick in place using a glue stick. Cut a piece of clear self-adhesive film slightly smaller than the front of the card, peel off the paper backing and press in place, to seal in the flowers and leaves.

219

Lovely Lavender

Have you got lavender growing in your yard? It is not only a pretty plant to look at but it is wonderfully perfumed – and butterflies and bees are attracted to it! At the end of the summer, it is a good idea to cut lavender back so it will be encouraged to grow even more flowers next year. Save all the stems that are cut off to make a lavender wand and a lavender sachet.

To make a lavender wand

You will need:
23 lavender stems
1¹/₂ yards narrow ribbon

1 Tie one end of the ribbon around the lavender stems, just below the heads.

2 Just below the point where you have tied the ribbon, bend each stem back over the heads.

3 Holding the bent stems loosely in one hand, take the long end of the ribbon and thread it in and out of the stems. Once you have gone round once, on the next row you will need to go over and under alternate stems, so the ribbon weaves in and out. When this weaving has completely covered the lavender heads, tie the ribbon round the stems. and fasten off with a bow.

To make a lavender sachet

You will need:
8 inch length of very
wide ribbon
sewing thread and needle
dried lavender
(see Crafty tip)
6 inch length of narrow ribbon

1 Fold the wide ribbon in half and stitch up both sides, to form a bag.

2 Fill the bag with lavender and tie with narrow ribbon.

Crafty tip
To dry lavender, tie in bunches and hang upside down for a few weeks, then rub the flowers off the stems, and store in an airtight container.

221

Crafty tip
If you do not have any ribbon, simply use some scraps of fabric. Sheer, thin fabrics are best, to allow the lovely lavender scent to come through.

Painted Pots

Why not use paints to decorate a few plain flower pots, transforming them into something bright and beautiful?

To make a painted pot

You will need:
terra-cotta flower pot
white emulsion paint
acrylic paints
soft paintbrush

1 Unless you want the original clay color of the pot to show through, first paint the pot white all over.

2 Now add some color! You could paint the main part of the pot and the rim in different colors, or paint a background color then add some stripes or another design.

Crafty tips
Painting the pot white to start with will help any subsequent colors to appear nice and bright. Instead of using white acrylic, use emulsion paint, which is a bit cheaper. Ask an adult – they may have some left after decorating the house.

Paint pot hanging basket

Ask a grown-up to save paint pots next time they are decorating. Large cans of emulsion are best, and they need to be thoroughly washed out before you start.

You will need:
clean, empty paint cans
acrylic paints
gravel, pebbles, or broken
clay pots
potting compost
plants, such as pansies

Painted twig

While you have your paints out, why not paint a twig to act as a plant support or simply to add a splash of color while you are waiting for flowers to bloom. If the bark is flaky, strip it off before painting your stick.

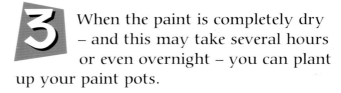

1 Paint the outside of the cans in a plain color. Black is a good choice as a single coat should easily cover up any words or pictures printed on the can.

2 When the first coat is dry, mix a bright color of acrylic paint with a little water to make a runny consistency – but not too runny.
Spread the paint thickly along the rim of the can, allowing it to drip down the outside.

3 When the paint is completely dry – and this may take several hours or even overnight – you can plant up your paint pots.

4 Put a layer of gravel, pebbles or broken clay pots in the base of your paint can. Then add compost, about two-thirds full. Add your plants and a little more compost, then hang up your paint can from its handle!

In the Kitchen

Contents

Introduction

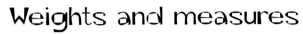

Eating is such a pleasure – especially when you have prepared the food yourself. Yes, cooking can be great fun and you are never too young to learn how to make delicious, nutritious snacks and meals.

Weights and measures

Use a weighing scales or measuring jug, where appropriate, and a ruler to measure pans. Small measurements are given in tsp (teaspoons) and tbsp (tablespoons).

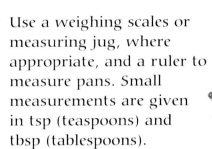

Try some of the recipes on these pages. There is sure to be something you fancy! How about a delicious dip, a home-made cake, warm from the oven, or even a simple sandwich? Stir up some soup, pack up a picnic, or prepare some great party food.

Just remember to put on your apron first, to protect your clothes, and clear up the kitchen after you have finished!

Basic equipment

Here is a list of the tools you will need. You should find most of them in your kitchen.

- medium-sized saucepan
- rectangular pan, 12in 8in
- round cake pan, 8in
- flat baking sheets
- measuring spoons
- mixing bowl
- wooden spoon

- whisk
- weighing scales
- metal skewer
- baking parchment or waxed paper
- strainer
- rolling pin

Cooking terms

There may be a few words and phrases you don't understand. Here are some but if you get stuck, a grown-up should have the answer!

- zest – the thinly cut peel of a lemon, orange, or lime. Make sure you cut off or grate just the colored part, not the white, bitter pith underneath.
- eggs – all the recipes on these pages use large sized eggs.
- butter gives a good flavor but you can substitute margarine, which is cheaper.
- all-purpose flour is used for most recipes. Where self-rising flour is needed, you can add baking powder to all-purpose flour. For bread, use a strong flour recommended for bread-making.

Delightful Dippers

Whip up a dip to enjoy with a packet of potato chips, some bread, or crunchy raw vegetable sticks. It's quick, it's healthy, and it's fun!

Salsa

This colorful dip could be served with potato or corn chips. It also makes a delicious accompaniment to burgers and hot dogs.

You will need:
2 tomatoes
2 scallions
half a cucumber
2 tbsp tomato relish
2 tbsp tomato catsup
salt and pepper
fresh cilantro, mint, or parsley
fresh vegetable sticks, to serve

1 Chop up the tomatoes, scallions and cucumber as small as you can. Put them in a bowl.

2 Stir in the tomato relish and tomato catsup, then season with salt and pepper.

3 Snip the fresh herbs into small pieces, using scissors, and stir into the dip just before serving.

228

Creamy cheese and onion dip

Mix together 2 tbsp each of natural yogurt, cream cheese, and mayonnaise. Add 1 tsp mustard and mix really well with a fork or whisk. Stir in 2 chopped scallions – or some chopped fresh herbs, if you prefer – and season with salt and pepper. Serve with raw vegetables such as bell peppers and celery, cut into sticks, or with pita bread, lightly broiled and cut into fingers.

Avocado dip

This Mexican-style dip, known as guacamole, can be served with corn chips, sometimes known as tortilla chips. Skin two ripe avocados and remove the stones, then mash up the flesh in a bowl. Stir in a tablespoon of tomato relish, two or three chopped scallions and the juice of a lime. To add a bit of spice, you can add a few drops of chili sauce, if you want. Stir in some chopped fresh cilantro leaves just before serving.

Snack Attack

These recipes are great for a light lunch or supper when you are quite hungry but don't want a big meal. Make enough for one, two, or more people!

Salmon fish cakes

This recipe will make six large fish cakes or eight medium-sized ones. Serve the fish cakes with a creamy cheese and onion dip, or with peas or baked beans.

You will need:
4 potatoes
1 tbsp butter
2 tbsp milk
7oz can of salmon
2 eggs
1 tbsp tomato catsup
dried breadcrumbs
salt and pepper
2 tbsp oil

1 Peel the potatoes, cut them into even-sized pieces, and place in a saucepan with enough cold water to cover. Place on the stove, over high heat, until the water boils, then put on a lid, turn down the heat, and cook for about 15 minutes, until soft. Test if the potatoes are done by poking with a skewer. Drain off the water and return the potatoes to the pan.

2 Mash the potatoes, adding the butter and milk. Leave to cool.

3 Drain the salmon and place it in a bowl. Break it up into small pieces with a fork. Add the potato and one of the eggs, the tomato catsup, and some salt and pepper and mix well until thoroughly blended.

4 Divide the mixture into six or eight equal portions. Shape each portion into a cake.

5 Beat the remaining egg in a shallow dish. Put the breadcrumbs in another dish.

6 Dip each fish cake into the egg, so it is coated all over, then into the breadcrumbs.

7 Heat the oil in a skillet and fry the fish cakes on both sides, until crisp and golden. Drain on kitchen paper towels before serving.

Alphabet soup

This smooth vegetable soup is made extra filling by adding pasta! Choose tiny pasta shapes such as alphabets or stars, or break spaghetti into short lengths. The soup will serve four people.

You will need:
2 onions
2 celery stalks
2 tbsp butter
1 tbsp oil
2 carrots
2 potatoes
2 tomatoes
1½ pints chicken or vegetable stock
about 1 cup pasta shapes

1 Peel and chop the onions. Chop the celery. Cook them in the oil and butter in a saucepan over medium heat for about 10 minutes, until soft.

2 Peel and chop the carrots and potatoes, and chop the tomatoes, then add to the pan. Cook, stirring, for 2 minutes, then pour in the stock.

3 Increase the heat until the soup starts to boil, then put a lid on the pan, reduce the heat to low, and leave to cook for 30 minutes.

231

4 Allow the soup to cool, then whizz it up, in a blender or food processor, until smooth. Return it to the pan and reheat over medium heat.

5 Cook the pasta in boiling salted water for 3 minutes, or according to the instructions on the packet. Drain and add to the soup.

cheesy toasts

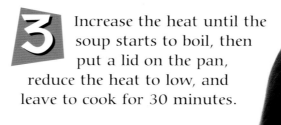

Grate ³/₄ cup Cheddar cheese and mix with 2 tsp mustard, 2 tbsp milk, and some salt and pepper. Toast two slices of bread under a hot broiler, on one side only, and spread the cheese mixture over the untoasted sides. Broil until the cheese is golden and bubbly.

Big Breakfast

The first meal of the day – and considered by some people to be the best! Treat yourself to something nourishing and your day will be off to a very good start!

Bacon bangers

Bacon and sausages are breakfast favorites – and they taste twice as nice when they are cooked together, like this! Instructions are given for baking the sausages in the oven but they could be fried or broiled, if you prefer.

You will need:
8 chipolata sausages
8 rashers of streaky bacon
1-2 tbsp oil

1 Heat the oven to 200°C/400°F.

2 Stretch the bacon rashers slightly and wrap one around each sausage.

3 Brush a baking sheet with oil and arrange the bacon-wrapped sausages on the sheet in a single layer. Cook in the oven for 20 minutes. Turn them over after 10 minutes. Serve with baked beans and broiled tomatoes.

Boiled egg and soldiers

A boiled egg is simple to cook and very delicious, especially with fingers of buttered toast for dipping! Pour water into a small saucepan so it is deep enough to cover the egg. Place the pan on the stove, over medium–high heat and, just before it starts to boil, carefully place the egg in the water. When the water starts to bubble, start timing! For a large egg, cook for 4 minutes for a set white and a runny yolk. Meanwhile, toast some bread. As soon as the time is up, hold the pan under the cold faucet for about 10 seconds, then transfer the egg to an egg cup. Butter the toast and cut it into fingers.

232

Muesli sundae

Muesli and yogurt is a healthy
breakfast option – and here's an idea
to make it look and taste extra special!
In a bowl, mix 3 tbsp muesli with 2 tbsp
orange or apple juice and 1 tsp runny honey.
Spoon half this mixture into a sundae glass;
then add a layer of yogurt. Add the rest of the
muesli and another layer of
yogurt and top with a
strawberry, or other
fruit, and a sprig of
fresh mint.

Scrambled eggs

To make perfect scrambled eggs for two people,
melt 2 tbsp butter in a saucepan over low
heat. Break four eggs into a bowl and add
2 tbsp milk and some salt and pepper.
Stir until well mixed, then add to the
pan. Cook over low heat, stirring all the
time. Be patient, as the eggs will take
about 10 minutes to cook.
You need to stir them so
they do not stick to the
pan, and so you end
up with really
creamy, soft
eggs. You can
stop stirring
just for long
enough to put
some bread in
the toaster or
under the
broiler. When
the eggs are
ready, divide them
between two serving
plates and add triangles
of buttered toast.

Brunch Munch

Here are some ideas for a late breakfast, perfect for a lazy weekend or vacation. Perhaps you could treat your parents to breakfast in bed?

American pancakes

This recipe makes about 12 pancakes – enough for two people or one very greedy one! You can spread the warm pancakes with butter and jelly, or serve them in a stack with some maple syrup and a wedge of lemon for squeezing!

You will need:
1 cup all-purpose flour
1 tsp baking soda
1 tsp superfine sugar
1 egg
$2/3$ cup milk
about 2 tbsp butter or 1-2 tbsp oil

1 Sift the flour with the baking soda into a mixing bowl. Stir in the sugar.

2 Make a hole in the center of the flour and add the egg. Beat the egg with a wooden spoon or whisk, allowing the flour to gradually become mixed in.

3 Add about a third of the milk and continue beating, allowing more flour to become mixed in.

4 Continue mixing, gradually adding the rest of the milk. When all the flour is incorporated, beat the mixture for about 2 minutes.

5 Place a non-stick or cast iron skillet over medium heat. Grease lightly with butter or oil. Using a large spoon or ladle, drop small puddles of batter into the pan. After a minute or so, bubbles will appear on the pancakes, then the bubbles will become holes. When these holes appear, the pancakes are ready to be turned over. Do this with a spatula. Cook for a further minute, then remove the pancakes from the pan. Repeat until all the batter has been used up.

Sweetcorn fritters

These can be eaten on their own, or with bacon or beans, and they are absolutely delicious! Instead of canned sweet corn you could use frozen corn which has been allowed to defrost.

You will need:
14oz can sweetcorn
1 egg
3-4 tbsp flour
salt and pepper
2 tbsp oil

1 Drain the corn and put it into a mixing bowl. Add the egg and mix well with a wooden spoon.

2 Add the flour and some salt and pepper. Mix well. The mixture should be quite thick, like porridge. If it seems too thin, add a little more flour.

3 Heat the oil in a skillet over medium heat. Using a large spoon or ladle, drop small puddles of mixture into the pan. Cook for a minute or two, until you can see the edges of the underside of the fritters turning golden brown, then turn them over with a spatula and cook for a further minute or two.

4 Remove the fritters from the pan and repeat until all the mixture has been used up. Serve with baked beans.

Fruit smoothie

In a blender, put a small banana, broken into chunks, and a 5fl oz carton of natural yogurt. Fill the empty yogurt carton with fruit juice – orange, apple, or pineapple – and pour into the blender. Then add your choice of fruit – a few raspberries, strawberries, or blueberries, perhaps, or a peach or pear peeled and cut into chunks. Whizz until smooth and pour into glasses. This is enough for two or three people.

Home-baked Bread

Home-baked bread is fun to make – mixing the dough, kneading it, shaping it into loaves or rolls, and watching it magically increase in size! And the smell of it baking is absolutely delicious! This dough can also be adapted to make the pizza recipes on the following pages.

Basic bread dough

You will need:
3 cups strong white bread flour
2 tsp salt
1 tsp superfine sugar
1 sachet of easy blend dried yeast
1¹/₂ cups warm water
1 egg

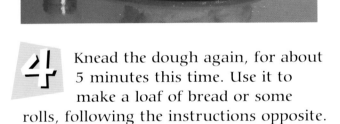

1 Put the flour, salt, half the sugar, and yeast in a large bowl, mix together, then stir in the warm water, using a wooden spoon. The dough should be soft and sticky.

2 Knead the dough on a floured surface for about 5-10 minutes. It should become less sticky and quite springy.

3 Place the dough in a lightly oiled plastic bag, put the bag in a bowl or on a baking sheet and leave in a warm place to rise for about 40 minutes. It should double in size!

4 Knead the dough again, for about 5 minutes this time. Use it to make a loaf of bread or some rolls, following the instructions opposite.

5 Place the loaf or rolls on a baking sheet which has been dusted with flour. Beat together the egg and the remaining sugar with 1 tsp water, and brush over the surface of the dough. Cover with a cloth and leave in a warm place for 30-40 minutes, to rise again.

6 Heat the oven to 230°C/450°F. Place the sheet of bread or rolls in the oven and bake for 20 minutes (for rolls) or 30 minutes (for a loaf). The bread is ready when it is golden and sounds hollow when you tap it with your knuckles. Transfer to a wire rack and leave to cool.

Speckled plait

The recipe for basic bread dough will make two loaves. Cut the dough in half then divide each half into three. Roll and stretch each piece into a long sausage and braid three sausages together. If you don't want to make a plait, just pat the dough into a loaf shape. When you have brushed the dough with the beaten egg mixture, you can sprinkle the top with poppy, sunflower, or sesame seeds.

Hedgehog rolls

The recipe for basic bread dough will make 12 rolls. Or you could use half to make a plaited loaf and the other half to make six rolls. Shape the rolls with your hands then, to make them, into hedgehogs, push peppercorns or cloves in place to make eyes, and snip the dough with scissors, to form prickles.

Perfect Pizza

To make pizza bases, follow the recipe for basic bread dough on the previous pages but leave out the sugar and add 2 tbsp olive oil with the water. Knead the dough for 10 minutes, place in an oiled plastic bag in a bowl in a warm place for about 40 minutes, until doubled in size, then follow the pizza recipes below.

Cheesy pizza

The pizza dough, made with 1lb flour, will be enough for two pizzas – just right for four hungry people or two very greedy ones! Use fresh tomato sauce or a jar of ready-made tomato pasta sauce. Instead of mozzarella cheese, you could use Cheddar, Edam, or another cheese.

You will need:
pizza dough (see above)
olive oil
tomato sauce
1 cup mozzarella cheese
black olives with stones removed
dried oregano
fresh basil leaves

238

1 Heat the oven to 230°C/450°F. Lightly grease two flat baking sheets with olive oil.

2 Take the risen dough from the bag and knead it on a floured surface for 2-3 minutes.

3 Divide the dough in half and place one half on each baking sheet. Press the dough with your fingers, flattening it out to make two pizza bases.

4 Spread each base with about 2-3 tbsp tomato sauce. Cut the cheese into slices and arrange on top, then decorate with olives, and sprinkle with oregano.

5 Bake the pizzas for 15 minutes, until the cheese has melted and the edges of the dough are crisp and golden. Sprinkle with fresh basil leaves.

Mini discs

Instead of two medium-sized pizzas, make four smaller ones. Each person could choose their own toppings, such as sliced mushrooms, drained canned tuna, or slices of salami.

239

French bread pizza

Cut a short loaf in half lengthways and brush the cut surface with a little olive oil. Add 2 tbsp tomato sauce, spreading it evenly over the bread, then add sliced or grated cheese. Top with thinly sliced salami and red bell pepper and a sprinkling of oregano.

Bake at 230°C/450°F for 15 minutes. Serve sprinkled with chopped fresh basil.

Packed Lunch

If you take your own lunch to school, here are some ideas you may not have tried yet. They are also great for a day out!

Birdie bars

These chewy bars, made from muesli, look a bit like birdseed! If you don't like coconut, add 1½ cups more muesli, or substitute some chopped nuts, sesame seeds, cherries, or chocolate chips!

1 Heat the oven to 150°C/300°F. Use a little bit of butter to grease a 12in x 10in shallow rectangular cake pan, or line the pan with baking parchment.

You will need:
1¼ cups butter
1½ cups muesli
½ cup light soft brown sugar
⅔ cups shredded coconut

2 Melt the rest of the butter in a saucepan over low heat.

3 Remove the pan from the heat and stir in the muesli, sugar, and coconut – or other ingredients of your choice.

4 Spoon the mixture into the pan and press it down evenly. Bake for 30–35 minutes, until set and golden.

5 Leave to cool for 5 minutes, then cut into bars – about 16!

Bean wraps

These make a nice change from ordinary sandwiches. You can buy wraps – otherwise known as flour tortillas – from supermarkets. Spread 1 tbsp mayonnaise over a tortilla, then put two lettuce leaves, shredded, in a line across the center, followed by 2 tbsp tomato relish, a little grated cheese, and about 2 tbsp drained, canned beans such as cannelini, borlotti, or red kidney beans. Season with salt and pepper, then roll up as tightly as you can, tucking in the sides as you go to seal in the filling. Cut in half and wrap in plastic wrap to keep it fresh until lunch time!

Chicken wraps

Follow the instructions for bean wraps but replace the beans and cheese with chopped, cooked chicken.

Sandwich fillings

Everyone has their own favorite fillings for sandwiches but sometimes you can get stuck for ideas. Here are some to try!
• Make a creamy cheese and onion dip to spread on slices of bread, then fill with shredded lettuce for added crunch! • Chop up a stick of celery and an apple and mix with 1/2 cup grated cheese. Add 1-2 tsp mayonnaise to bind the mixture together. • Drain a can of tuna or salmon and mash up with 1 tbsp mayonnaise and 1 tsp tomato catsup. • Spread bread slices with peanut butter and add slices of banana, then drizzle with runny honey!

Fruit salad pots

To make a balanced lunch, add a pot full of fresh fruit! Peel and chop a kiwi fruit and place in a plastic pot with strawberries, redcurrants, blueberries, or whatever fruit is in season. Put on the lid and don't forget to pack a spoon. It couldn't be easier!

241

Picnic Time

When you are packing a picnic, it's nice to have something tempting to eat, so you can enjoy your lunch, whatever the weather!

Sticky chicken wings

Ask a grown-up to cut each chicken wing in half, before you start, by snipping through the joint in the middle. If you can't find chicken wings in the stores, use chicken drumsticks, which are slightly larger and so will need another 10-15 minutes' cooking time.

1 In a large bowl, mix together the cola, sugar, catsup, mustard, and Worcestershire sauce, and season with salt and pepper.

2 Add the prepared chicken wings and leave to marinate for 1 hour.

3 About 10 minutes before you start to cook the chicken, heat the oven to 200°C/400°F.

4 Arrange the chicken pieces in a single layer on a baking sheet. Cook for 20 minutes, then turn each one over, using tongs, and cook for a further 20 minutes.

You will need:
2lb chicken wings
half can of cola
2 tbsp dark soft brown sugar
4 tbsp tomato catsup
1 tbsp mustard
few drops of Worcestershire sauce
salt and pepper

5 To check that the chicken is cooked, pierce with a skewer or the tip of a knife. The juices should run clear. If the juice and the flesh inside the chicken wing is pink, cook for a further 5 minutes and test again.

6 Eat the chicken wings hot, or leave to cool and refrigerate before packing them in your picnic basket!

Shortcrust pastry

You will need:
1 1/2 cups all-purpose flour
1 tsp salt
1/2 cup butter, margarine, or lard
2 tbsp cold water

1 Sift the flour and salt into a large mixing bowl.

2 Cut the butter, margarine, or lard into small pieces and add to the bowl. Using your fingertips, rub the fat into the flour. You should end up with a mixture that looks like fresh breadcrumbs.

3 Sprinkle the water into the bowl and gather the dough together in your hands. You should be able to squeeze it into a large ball. Sprinkle a little flour on your work surface and knead the dough for one or two minutes. Keep it in a plastic bag in the refrigerator for up to two days until you are ready to use it.

Half-moon pasties

You can buy shortcrust pastry already made. You can even buy it already rolled out! If you want to make your own pastry, use the recipe above!

You will need:
4 potatoes
1lb shortcrust pastry
flour
2 scallions
1/2 cup cheese, grated
salt and pepper
1 egg

1 Heat the oven to 200°C/400°F.

2 Peel the potatoes and cut into small cubes. Place in a saucepan with enough cold water to cover, bring to the boil, then reduce the heat, and simmer for 5 minutes. Drain and leave to cool.

3 Dust your work surface with flour. Divide the pastry in half and roll out each half to a circle the size of a dinner plate.

4 Chop the scallions and mix with the potatoes. Add the cheese and season with salt and pepper. Divide the mixture between the two pastry circles.

5 Beat the egg with 1 tsp water and brush the edges of the pastry circles with this mixture. Fold each circle in half, enclosing the potato filling. Press down the edges, to seal them. To make a decorative edge, make small cuts all around the edge of the pastry and fold over each little tab. Brush the pastry all over with egg mixture and cut three slits in the top of each pasty.

6 Place the pasties on baking sheets and bake for 30 minutes, until golden.

243

Faster Pasta

Pasta is quick to cook and satisfyingly filling to eat! Here are some quick and easy ideas to enjoy at snack time, dinner time, or party time!

Fresh tomato sauce

This sauce can be used with any pasta or as a pizza topping. The recipe makes enough for four servings and it can be kept in the refrigerator for up to three days, in a covered container, and reheated when you need it.

You will need:
1 large onion, peeled
2 celery stalks
2 tbsp olive oil
8 ripe tomatoes
4 tbsp tomato purée
4 tbsp water
salt and pepper
fresh basil (optional)

1 Chop the onion and celery into very small pieces. Heat the oil in a saucepan over medium heat and cook the chopped onion and celery for about 10 minutes, stirring frequently, until it is soft and golden.

2 Chop the tomatoes, add them to the pan and cook for a further 2 minutes, then stir in the tomato purée and water.

3 Cook the sauce for a further 10 minutes, then add seasoning.

4 Just before serving, add some chopped fresh basil leaves, if you like.

Easy peasy tuna pasta

This recipe is enough for four people. If you don't like tuna, substitute some chopped, cooked chicken or ham or, for a vegetarian dish, some cheese, cut into cubes.

You will need
2 cups pasta shells
salt and pepper
150ml carton of light cream
2 tbsp tomato purée
2 tbsp canned sweetcorn
about 12 stuffed green olives
200g can tuna
2 tbsp grated Parmesan cheese

1 Boil plenty of water in a large saucepan, adding a pinch of salt. When the water is boiling, add the pasta shells and cook them for 8 minutes, or according to the instructions on the packet.

2 Drain and return the pasta to the saucepan over low heat. Stir in the cream, tomato purée, and sweetcorn. Slice the olives and stir these in, too. Add the tuna.

3 Transfer the pasta to a serving dish and sprinkle with Parmesan cheese.

245

Spaghetti in a hurry

Cook spaghetti according to the instructions on the packet. Cooked meatballs, diced grilled bacon and sliced sausages are all good with spaghetti and delicious with fresh tomato sauce (see recipe on opposite page). Simmer the sauce with the meat gently for about 10 minutes until heated right through and spoon over the drained spaghetti.

Super Salad Bar

Salads are not just summer food – and not just a side dish, either. What's more, they are an enjoyable way to eat really healthy stuff!

Fruity coleslaw

This is a lovely, crunchy salad, quite different from the coleslaw you buy in tubs in the supermarket. Serve it with other salads or as an accompaniment to burgers or sausages. It's a great way to eat up your cabbage!

You will need:
14oz white cabbage
2 carrots
2 oranges
1/3 cup golden raisins
3 tbsp mayonnaise or salad cream
salt and pepper

1 Slice the cabbage thinly – you may need the help of an adult – and it will fall into shreds. Put these in a mixing bowl.

2 Peel the carrots and grate them. Add to the cabbage.

3 Peel the orange and cut into segments. Do this on a plate so you can save any juice that comes out. Add the orange segments and the golden raisins to the cabbage and carrot.

4 Spoon the mayonnaise or salad cream into a cup and add the orange juice and some salt and pepper. Whisk together with a fork and pour over the salad. Mix well.

Greek salad

Feta cheese and olives give this salad a salty flavor and the tomatoes, bell peppers and cucumber add sweetness and crunch. You could use any colored peppers. You can also add some chopped onion, if you like.

You will need:
1 cup feta cheese
4 tomatoes
half a cucumber
1 green bell pepper
$^1/_3$ cup black olives, stones removed
salad dressing (see right)

1 Cut the cheese into small cubes and put these in a bowl.

2 Cut the tomatoes into quarters and add to the cheese.

3 Cut the cucumber into small chunks and add to the bowl.

4 Cut the bell pepper in half and remove the stalk, the seeds, and any white pieces. Cut the pepper into small slices and add to the bowl.

5 Add the olives and pour on some dressing – about 2 tbsp. Mix well and serve.

Salad dressing

This is a basic oil and vinegar dressing, flavored with mustard. You can use red or white wine vinegar, or cider vinegar, or any other kind of vinegar you like. You can use smooth French mustard, or grainy mustard, or hot English mustard. And you may choose to use olive oil or sunflower oil. It's up to you!

Use a fork to whisk together 2 tsp vinegar and 1 tsp mustard in a small bowl or cup. Add 7 tsp oil and whisk again. Season with salt and pepper. Use the dressing immediately or transfer it to a clean jam jar or bottle and store in the refrigerator for up to a week.

To make a larger quantity of dressing, use a tablespoon instead of a teaspoon!

247

Tea Party Treats

These treats are perfect for a birthday tea! Just add a few bowls of potato chips and you'll have a celebratory feast!

Marshmallow jellies

You will need:
1 packet raspberry jelly
150ml natural yogurt
$1/2$ cup mini marshmallows
chocolate sprinkles

1 Boil some water in a kettle. Meanwhile, break up the jelly into cubes and place these in a heatproof measuring jug.

2 Pour boiling water into the jug until the liquid reaches the 14fl oz mark. Stir until the jelly cubes dissolve. Leave to cool slightly.

3 Whisk the yogurt into the cooled jelly, using a fork, until well blended. Pour into four sundae glasses and sprinkle marshmallows on top of each one. Chill in the refrigerator until set – about 2-3 hours.

4 Before serving, top with chocolate sprinkles.

Pinwheel sandwiches

Spread 1 tbsp mayonnaise or cream cheese over a soft flour tortilla (or wrap). Add two lettuce leaves, cut into shreds, and a slice of ham, chopped, or some grated cheese. Roll up tightly and cut into slices before arranging on a serving plate with some parsley leaves to garnish.

chocolate cookie bars

This recipe combines white and milk chocolate with sweet, crunchy cookie pieces. It also contains candied peel but if you don't like the taste of this, use chopped dried apricots instead, or just add more cherries – red, yellow, and green – and golden raisins.

You will need
9oz graham crackers
1/3 cup candied peel
1/4 cup glacé cherries
1/2 cup golden raisins
11oz white chocolate
4 tbsp milk
4oz milk chocolate

1 Break the crackers into small pieces and put them in a mixing bowl.

2 Snip the peel into small pieces, using scissors, and add to the crackers. Add the cherries and golden raisins.

3 Break the white chocolate into pieces and put them, with the milk, in a heatproof bowl. Place the bowl on top of a saucepan with some hot water in it and set the pan over low heat until the chocolate has melted. Alternatively, melt the chocolate and milk in a microwave.

4 Pour the melted chocolate over the cracker mixture and mix well.

5 Line a 12in x 8in pan with baking parchment and put the mixture in the pan, pressing it down firmly all over.

6 Melt the milk chocolate and, using a teaspoon, drizzle it over the cracker mixture.

7 Place the pan in the refrigerator for about 2 hours, until set, then cut into 16 bars.

249

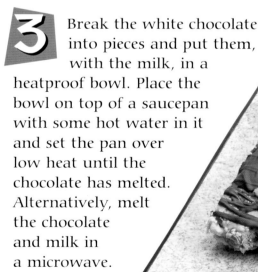

Food for Friends

Add a salad to the recipes on this page and you have a great meal to serve to friends or family!

Meatballs

These can be eaten hot or cold. Hot, they are great with pasta or cold, speared on toothpicks, they can be served with delicious dip.

You will need:
1 onion
1lb minced beef
1 egg
1 tbsp dried breadcrumbs
salt and pepper
oil

1 Finely chop or grate the onion and mix with the meat.

2 Lightly beat the egg and add it to the meat mixture. Mix in well, then add the breadcrumbs and season with salt and pepper.

3 Using your hands, form the mixture into 24 balls.

4 Pour enough oil into a skillet to coat the base. Fry the meatballs over medium heat, turning frequently, until they are brown all over. Drain on kitchen paper towels.

Garlic and herb bread

Mash 1 tbsp butter with a crushed garlic clove and a sprinkling of dried herbs such as thyme or oregano. Slice a French stick and butter both sides of each slice with the garlic and herb butter. Wrap in aluminum foil and bake for 10 minutes at 200°C/400°F.

Lemon and banana trifles

You will need:
8 sponge fingers
2 small bananas
1 lemon jelly
cream
hundreds and thousands

1 Break up the sponge fingers and divide the pieces equally between four sundae glasses.

2 Boil some water in a kettle. Meanwhile, break up the jelly into cubes and place these in a heatproof measuring jug.

3 Pour boiling water into the jug until the liquid reaches the 14fl oz mark. Stir until the jelly cubes dissolve, then add cold water to make 1 pint. Leave to cool slightly.

4 Chop up the bananas and add the pieces to the sundae glasses. Pour in the jelly, then place the glasses in the refrigerator until the jelly has set – about 2-3 hours.

5 Just before serving, top each trifle with cream and sprinkle with hundreds and thousands.

Lime refresher

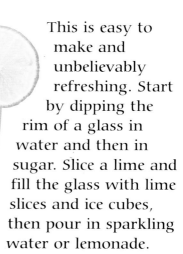

This is easy to make and unbelievably refreshing. Start by dipping the rim of a glass in water and then in sugar. Slice a lime and fill the glass with lime slices and ice cubes, then pour in sparkling water or lemonade.

251

Baking Day

On a rainy afternoon, bake a batch of cookies and fill the house with delicious cooking aromas!

Brownies

These little squares are chewy with a wonderful crisp crust on top. If you don't like walnuts, use almonds or another kind of nut. Replace nuts with chocolate chunks, if you prefer chocolate or if you have a nut allergy.

1 Heat the oven to 180°C/350°F. Line a 12in x 8in cake pan with baking parchment.

2 Break the chocolate into pieces and put them, with the butter, in a heatproof bowl. Place the bowl on top of a saucepan with some hot water in it and set the pan over low heat until the chocolate and butter have melted. Alternatively, melt the chocolate and butter in a microwave.

3 In a separate bowl, beat together the eggs, sugar, and vanilla.

4 Pour the melted chocolate into the egg mixture and whisk until well blended.

You will need:
9oz plain chocolate
1 cup walnut pieces
1 cup butter
4 eggs
1 1/2 cups superfine sugar
1 tsp vanilla extract
1 cup all-purpose flour
salt

5 Add the flour and a pinch of salt and gently stir into the chocolate mixture. Stir in the nuts.

6 Pour the mixture into the pan and bake for 35 minutes, until the top is crisp and pale.

7 Remove from the oven, leave to cool for 10 minutes, then transfer the cake to a wire rack, to finish cooling. Cut into 24 squares.

Gingerbread people

If you do not have a cookie cutter in the shape of a person, you could use any shape you like – stars, animals, circles, whatever you have available! Instead of making your own icing, you can buy colored icing in little tubes – quick and easy to use!

You will need:
1/3 cup butter
1/2 cup superfine sugar
2 tbsp golden syrup
1 cup all-purpose flour
2 tsp ground ginger
1/2 tsp baking soda
50g confectioner's sugar
2 tsp water

1 Heat the oven to 180°C/350°F. Use a little of the butter to grease two flat baking sheets, or line them with baking parchment.

2 Put the butter, sugar, and syrup in a saucepan and heat very gently, stirring with a wooden spoon, until melted.

3 Sift the flour, ginger, and baking soda into a large bowl.

4 Make a hole in the center of the flour and pour in the melted ingredients. Mix well with a wooden spoon, until you have a firm dough.

5 Roll out the dough on a board dusted with flour, until it is 1/4in thick. Use a cutter to cut out shapes and lift each one carefully on to the prepared baking sheets.

6 Bake for 10–12 minutes, then transfer to a wire rack and leave to cool.

7 Mix the confectioner's sugar with water, spoon it into a piping bag, and pipe patterns on to the cookies.

253

Cakes

Bake a delicious cake and everyone will want to be invited to tea!

Lemon yogurt cake

This is a low-fat recipe which makes it healthier than a lot of other cakes – and just as delicious!

254

You will need:
a little vegetable oil
5fl oz natural yogurt
grated zest of 1 lemon
1 1/4 cups superfine sugar
2 eggs
1 3/4 self-rising flour
1 cup confectioner's sugar
juice of half a lemon

1 Heat the oven to 180°C/350°F. Use the vegetable oil to grease a 2lb loaf pan. Line the pan with waxed paper or baking parchment.

2 Put the yogurt in a large bowl with the lemon zest and sugar.

3 Break the eggs into a small bowl and, using a wooden spoon, beat them lightly, then add them gradually to the yogurt mixture, beating all the time. Add the flour and beat again.

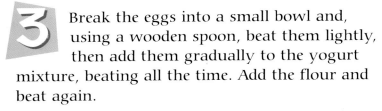

4 Pour the mixture into the cake pan and bake for 45 minutes. To test if the cake is done, push a skewer into the center. If it comes out clean, the cake is ready. If there is some cake mixture sticking to it, return the cake to the oven, bake for a further 5 minutes, and test again.

5 Transfer the cake to a wire rack, peel off the paper and leave to cool.

6 Meanwhile, mix the confectioner's sugar with the lemon juice. Spread over the top of the cooled cake.

Cup cakes

Bake these doll-sized cakes in small paper cases – there's enough mixture for about 20 – then decorate with frosting and colored sprinkles.

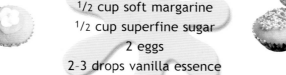

You will need:
1 cup self-rising flour
$^1/_2$ cup soft margarine
$^1/_2$ cup superfine sugar
2 eggs
2-3 drops vanilla essence

 1 Heat the oven to 180°C/350°F. Arrange 20 double paper cases on a baking sheet.

2 Sift the flour into a large bowl. Add all the other ingredients and beat with a wooden spoon until evenly blended.

 3 Spoon the mixture into the paper cases and bake for 15 minutes, until springy to the touch.

4 Place the cakes on a wire rack and leave to cool.

Decorations

To make frosting, mix together 250g confectioner's sugar with 2-3 tsp water. Add a few drops of food coloring, if you wish, and spread a little frosting on top of each cake. Then add sugar strands and other edible decorations.

255

Lemon yogurt cake decorating ideas

You could use lemon jelly slices to decorate the cake, or strips of lemon peel. Or add stripes of yellow frosting while the white icing is still soft, and run a skewer through, to create a pattern.

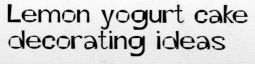

Project Notes